British School of Millinery
Tiara Headdresses

DENISE INNES-SPENCER

First published in the United Kingdom in 2017 by The British School of Millinery

Produced by The Choir Press

ISBN 978-0-9957872-0-9

Front cover picture and Chapter 7: Kathleen photographed by Frozen Visions

Dedicated to Richard, Samuel, Faith, Isobel and Megan, who I live for, and who constantly support me.

To my hardworking colleagues Sue, Gemma, Emily, Heidi and Helen, without whom this book would not have been written.

To Fiona Castle, who stood by me when times were hard. You had immense faith in me when I could not see it myself. You knew there was a plan and I can see that now.

And to my beautiful mother Kathleen, who died before she could see this book published. Thank you, Mum.

Thank you!

Contents

Foreword by Tracy Connop and Bridget Bailey   9

Preface   11

Introduction   13

Chapter 1: Equipment and Materials   15
    Basic tools   15
    Wires for use in tiaras   16
    Using knitted wire for headdresses   18
    Fastenings to the head   20
    Decoration   22

Chapter 2: Face Shapes   25
    Head measurements   25
    Face shapes   26
    Headdress styles suitable for various face shapes   27

Chapter 3: Basic Techniques   30
    Stitches   30
    Denise's handmade tiara headband   33
    Covering a headband with knitted wire   35
    Making a simple wire base   38
    Grip wire   42
    Creating a design guide   43
    Extending the comb   45
    Attaching the comb   47
    Ribbon loops   48
    Setting stones   50

Chapter 4: Beaded Tiaras   52
    Wire and beads (beaded tiara methods)   52
    Megan (twisted pearl)   53
    Jessica (threaded through weaving)   56

Chapter 5: Using Stones with Wire   62
    Isobel (tiara with acrylic stones)   63
    Introduction to Swarovski stones   69
    Faith (headband with Swarovski stones)   70

Chapter 6: Making Wired Fabric from Scratch   75

Louise (freestyle scrunching)   76

Rachel (teardrop-shaped headpiece)   81

Chapter 7: Working with Knitted Wire and Cup Chain   86

Kathleen (knitted wire base headpiece)   87

Lois (knitted wire tiara)   93

Chapter 8: Broken Jewellery, Brooches and Buttons   100

Helen (small hair combs)   100

Lady Mary (hair pins)   103

Chapter 9: Hair Vines   108

Polly (flower hair vine)   108

India (forehead bandeau of knitted wire)   114

Brands   120

Suppliers List   121

Bibliography   122

Acknowledgements   123

Further Thanks   126

Foreword

BY TRACY CONNOP AND BRIDGET BAILEY

I have asked two people to do the foreword to this book for a reason. Designing a headdress for a wedding dress is a two-way street. The designer of the dress has a vision for the style of headdress that would go with the dress, whilst the headdress/tiara designer also has a vision of what they think would be good for the trend, the style of the dress and, importantly, what would suit the face shape of the individual bride.

I asked Tracy Connop how she works with a headdress maker, and Bridget Bailey of Bailey Tomlin how she chooses a headdress to complement an outfit.

As a bridalwear designer I know, of course, how important the wedding gown is on the day, but it's not just about the dress; it's the 'whole look', including the tiara and veil.

This book, *British School of Millinery Tiara Headdresses*, is a must for all brides-to-be. Yes, there are a myriad of designs to choose from out there, but the joy of now being able to create your own special headpiece is amazing.

British School of Millinery Tiara Headdresses is superb. From a designer's perspective, the projects included in this book are not only beautifully designed, but the instructions are very simple and concise, making them easy enough for even an absolute beginner to make.

British School of Millinery Tiara Headdresses should be on every bride-to-be's list.

Tracy Connop
Bridal wear designer

I've known Denise for over 20 years while training with Rose Cory. Denise has a mass of experience making couture millinery, working in the industry and teaching, and she brings it all to this book. With inspiring designs and clear instructions, it's a great and generous thing that she is now sharing her skills. Lucky milliners!

Bridget Bailey
Bailey Tomlin

One project from each Chapter has been trialled by the British School of Millinery's own part-time students. I also asked some absolute beginners. Each student had two weeks to read, digest and make their item. None of them had seen the projects in advance and none of them knew what was expected of them until they opened the envelope. By doing this and getting their reactions I hope I have shown how easy it is to make some of the items. Also, from a personal perspective, the students have shown me that I can develop more challenging projects in future books!

Preface

Ever since I started teaching I have wanted to write books and share my knowledge. When I started out, there was very little information on the skills needed in tiara making, and what did exist was incomplete. So I just practised and practised and spent many nights working on perfecting my skills. Little did I know then where this would lead.

Today I find myself involved in the craft skills debate. At Cheltenham Literature Festival I sat beside Professor Roger Kneebone of Imperial College London demonstrating the same stitch – he was demonstrating a skin join whilst I was working in felt! I was humbled by this incredibly talented surgeon, but likewise he was full of admiration for the skills that we as milliners have. The stents that are used to hold open major arteries are the same tubular knitted wire that I use as the basis for my tiaras. Sounds odd but it is true. It seems that the knowledge given to the surgeons in the 17th and 18th centuries has now gone full circle and milliners are now using what the surgeons and scientists have made. I am so proud to be part of this circle.

Loving millinery as I do, I hope this book inspires you and in doing so keeps these traditional skills alive.

A thought from the past: in 1982, Trev Newby, a close friend of mine, said, 'One day you will write a book about everything you know about sewing.' It turns out that I know more than enough for one book. Here is the first book of the series!

Introduction

I have always been impressed by these quotations about millinery:

Milliners never seem to have any difficulty discovering geometrical shapes wholly unknown to mathematicians.

Evan Esar

All good hats are made of nothing.

Oscar Wilde, a man who knew a hat well!

(*The Hat Book*, Rodney Smith and Leslie Smolan, New York: Doubleday)

I work in an industry with a 4,000-year history, where the use of mercury once made madness an occupational hazard. Whilst technology has inevitably changed what milliners can do with fabrics, the basic processes remain the same. Skills developed and practised in the past still resonate in milliners' work today.

As a designer, I am always on the lookout for new and innovative materials to work with. Most recently this has been the use of knitted wire manufactured for the medical industry. I have experimented by manipulating and transforming this innovative product, used in surgery for stents, into flowers and headdresses including a headdress for jazz musician Paloma Faith. New materials like this constantly challenge me as a designer to think outside the box, developing new techniques.

Chapter 1

Equipment and Materials

Basic tools

Every maker has their own equipment that they prefer to use. I am no exception.

I need to have the tools that I want to use with me on every project. The set-up costs are very small. In fact, all these tools (apart from a few small pieces) can be bought from any hardware store or hobby-craft shop.

Hard-working tools

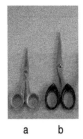

a   b

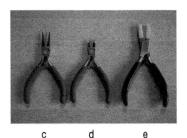

c   d   e

a. Small sharp scissors
b. Old scissors for cutting wire (the wire will blunt your scissors, so you must keep a separate pair)

c. Round-nose pliers
d. Flat back wire cutters
e Nylon jaw pliers

Sewing tools

f   g   h i j k l   m

f. A selection of Straw needles (sizes from 3 to 9)
g. Pins long
h. Tape measure/ruler
i. Fine felt-tip pen (red)
j. Fine felt-tip pen (black)

k. A pencil or small round piece of 5mm dowel
l. Nail file
m. All-purpose glue (or similar clear-drying craft glue)

Layout tools

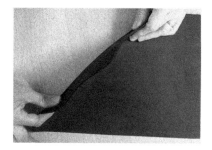

n. Compressed foam mat bought from a hobby shop. Used for pinning into to stop items moving. Also used for setting stones with the rhinestone setter as a buffer

Setting tools

o. Rhinestone setter, used for setting stones in sew-in clamps. I use two types. One is the clamp I have used for years (the black and red clamp with three sizes of stone), which is twenty years old and no longer in production. The clamping tool beside it is the new version and can be purchased from Creative Beadcraft (details under 'Suppliers List' in the back of the book)

Wires for use in tiaras

The first thing you need to know is what the different wires will do. The varied weights and widths have different capabilities, so it's good to read this section before you start. As I have been making tiaras for many years, I have learned which wires to use when.

Wires can be sold on plastic reels or in coils which must be unravelled carefully to avoid ending up with a bird's nest of tangled wires. See pictures below.

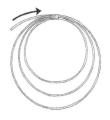

How to undo wire when coiled

All wires are measured by gauges: the thickness of the wire.

0.1 0.2 0.4 0.6 0.8 1.0 1.2

From left to right, looking at the picture:

0.1mm wire, known as a wrapping/stitching wire, is the finest wire that can be used. It has the appearance of hair and can break very easily. It is used for sewing and some lightweight attaching of wires, such as on fine knitted wire tube. Can be used for lightweight scrunching. Not used for construction. Available in many colours, this wire can be cut with scissors and wire cutters.

In the colour silver, for all the following sizes, I always buy the non-tarnish wire.

0.2mm wire, also known as a wrapping/stitching wire. I find this is the most-used wire of the selection. It is mainly used for sewing and some lightweight construction. Can sew on heavy stones and glass beads. This can also be used to mark centre lines by sewing, for plotting the design. Can be used for scrunching (see Chapter 6). Available in many colours, this wire can be cut with craft scissors and wire cutters.

0.4mm wire, known as a wrapping/binding wire, is used for lightweight to medium-weight work. A wire that is used for sewing and construction, this is used in conjunction with 0.6mm wire and both work together well. This wire will hold secure wires that are used for construction. Could be used for heavyweight scrunching. Available in many colours, it is recommended that this be cut with craft scissors or wire cutters.

0.6mm wire, known as a structure/construction wire and a lightweight base wire. Can be used to support all the knitted wires when using elastic on 1920s headbands, but used mainly with the tight knit 0.1mm wire and for hair vines (see Chapter 9). Available in many colours, it is recommended that this be cut with wire cutters.

0.8mm wire is a heavyweight structure/construction wire used when you want to have more support. I use this wire when the 0.6mm does not provide enough support and the 1.0mm is too heavy. This wire bends into intricate shapes which the 1.0mm won't do. Available in many colours, it is recommended that this be cut with wire cutters.

1.0mm wire is a lightweight foundation wire. Used for children's headbands and constructions that require unusual and intricate shapes. I use this wire with 1.2mm wire when I need firm but heavier shapes. Available in many colours, it is recommended that this be cut with wire cutters.

1.2mm wire is a heavyweight foundation wire. It is used in the adult headband wire with 0.4mm wire for wrapping. Everything you make for the head must be based either on this wire or on 1.5mm wire, but the 1.2mm wire is the most used for this. Available in many colours, it is recommended that this be cut with wire cutters.

Using knitted wire for headdresses

The first thing you must learn is how to manipulate the metal fabric. The fabric needs a pair of craft scissors that are just for knitted fabric, as it will blunt scissors. The needles that you use must only be for this fabric too. I keep all the tools that I use for this fabric separate from my other millinery tools.

There are five sizes of wire in the pre-knitted wire range. The wire comes in many colours, but some of them can be bright and gaudy and it can be difficult to colour match wires from different companies.

a. **85mm wide 0.1mm tight knit wire** comes in many colours and is used for tiara bases that are wider and longer. This is quite a delicate wire that should only be used for bases without heavy stones or beads. This can be used as a lining. As with the 15mm, be careful when you sew on it as it tends to pull and catch. This wire can be cut with craft scissors.

b. **15mm wide 0.1mm tight knit wire** comes in many colours and is used for tiara bases that are thin and slim. It is quite a delicate wire that should only be used for bases without heavy stones or beads. This can also be used as a lining, as I have done in 'India' in Chapter 9. You need to be careful when you sew on it as it tends to pull and catch. This wire can be cut with craft scissors.

c. **85mm wide 0.2mm coarse knitted wire** comes in many colours. Used for tiara bases that are wider and longer. This is quite a strong wire that can be used for bases with heavier stones or beads. Does not pull and catch. Used as a double layer, this can take heavier stones. This is not suitable as a lining. This wire can be cut with craft scissors.

The next two are relatively new wires that can be used in 'Polly' and 'India' in Chapter 9.

d

d. **20mm wide 0.1mm ultra-fine knitted tube.** Comes in limited colours, some of which do match the colours of the knitted wire. Great for supporting wire and hiding the wires inside. This wire can be cut with craft scissors. This can be used as a lining.

e

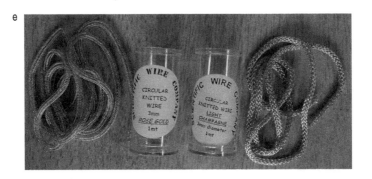

e. **0.1X 3mm tight knit circular knitted wire.** Comes in limited colours, some of which do match the colours of the above knitted wire tube in-d. Great for supporting wire and hiding the wires inside. This wire can be cut with craft scissors.

f. **Perl** is a coiled wire that is normally used in military uniforms as braiding for epaulettes. This fabric can be a brilliant addition to hair vines. Made from either 1.2mm (g) or 1.9mm (i) wire, it is tightly spiralled together, making a coil which is hollow. Through the hollow you can feed wire that when finished can make beautiful hair vines, and with multiple layers of perl these can be directed in different places on the head. 1.2mm wire can be stretched, and threading wire of a contrasting colour through the coil can be another way of adding colour, as used in Chapter 9.

g

ga

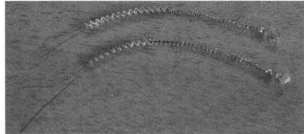

gb

g. **Bullion** is a similarly coiled wire (ga), sometimes as a tube, sometimes as a twisted tube that looks effective. Made of 0.2mm wire for the plain bullion, this again can be stretched and have a contrasting colour threaded through the coil (gb). The twisted version (g) is made from a flattened 0.1mm tape that helps the twist form its shape, as used in Chapter 4.

Fastenings to the head

Hair pins, with loops

a. This is a normal hair pin with loops at the curve of the pin. It is used for buns and chignons. Can be joined together as in 'Lady Mary' in Chapter 8.

Combs

a

b c d

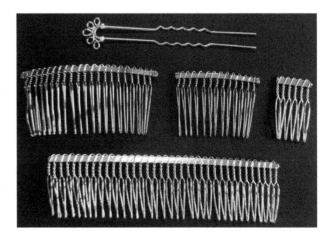

e

Metal ones are the best to use. They come in four sizes:

a. 2 pronged hair pin, 5 loops for decoration
b. 8cm (standard size used for flowers and large decorative pieces)
c. 6cm (small headdress combs)
d. 2cm (hair combs)
e. 13.5cm (used for veil headdresses and mounting lace pieces)

In the 1990s we only had plastic combs and there were no holes in them to sew on the decoration. Poking holes in them with a hot needle was a bit of a hard task. With the new metal combs, you can extend the combs (see Chapter 3) or sew straight onto the bars, which tend to be thinner than the old plastic combs.

Headbands

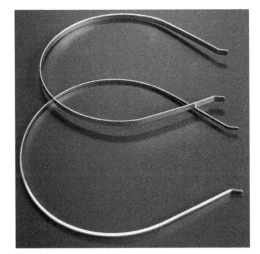

5mm gold headband

3mm silver headband

A thick piece of metal tape that is bent into the shape of a head. These come in various widths, but I prefer 3mm and 5mm because they can be hidden better in the hair.

Ribbon loops (Jump rings)

Round loops (usually a jump ring used in jewellery making) that are attached to the sides of a tiara or headdress. Easy to attach and used with ribbon to tie.

Grip wire

A bar of strong wire that is attached to a headdress or a side tiara. Using a stronger gauge wire (0.6mm, 0.8mm, 1.0mm), you can make these in Chapter 6.

Decoration

Glass bicones

Various beads made of metal and glass. I use only metal and glass beads that are suitable for tiaras. I prefer this kind because of their quality; I find many plastic beads look very cheap.

AB cut glass beads

Glass beads sold in packets

The facets on these beads are cut to reflect light and reflect off other cut glass pieces. These are sold in strings of 25.

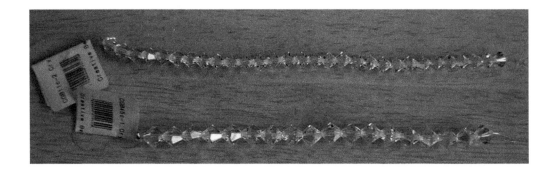

Pre-made metal pieces

I normally buy metal pieces from card decoration websites, where they generally cost less than from companies specifically selling for the tiara market.

Cup chain and Diamante stones with settings

Diamante chain and cup chain can be expensive; please see the suppliers list in the back of the book. It is good to shop around for your supplies. The pre-set stones are the best to use as they save time. However, the larger stones are available from Swarovski; again, see the suppliers list.

Rondelles and Shamballa-style balls are always good for tiaras. A bindi-drop style also works well for headbands and beaded tiaras.

Most of the sew-in stones have holes on each side of the stone bases.

Flowers

Here is an example of how I strip ready-made flowers to put on a headdress. In my headdresses, I strip the flower to a minimum (taking off leaves and decoration, see below) and use only what's needed. This helps the headdress to be lighter and avoid extra bulk.

I hope all the tips I have given you within this Chapter will help you to make your tiaras and headdresses.

Chapter **2**
Face Shapes

In this Chapter I will guide you through which headdresses suit each face shape. I will begin with how to measure a head and determine your face shape. This will then allow you to select the style of headdress that will best complement your or your customer's face shape.

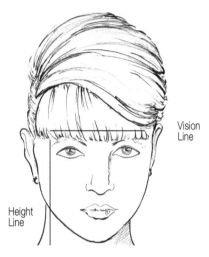

Vision Line

Height Line

Head measurements

1. **Vision line:** this is the width between eyebrows, from outside edge to outside edge, and determines the maximum width a tiara should be.
2. **Height line:** this is the length between the eyebrows and the chin. The height of the tiara should not exceed this measurement.
3. **Circumference:** around the head above the eyebrows and ears, including the largest part of the skull at the back.
4. **Back of the head:** needed for hair vines, this is the distance around the largest part of the skull found directly behind and between each ear.
5. **Over the head ear to ear:** from the tip of the ear over the head to the tip of the other ear. This measurement is used for the depth of crowns.

The rule for face shapes is 'whatever happens in the chin area and within the face shape happens on the crown area'. This gives a sense of balance and proportion.

| Round | Circlet or diadem on halo |

| Heart | Apex, soft with curves |

(with permission Annie Johnston)

| Diamond | Gable, sharp with angles |

(with permission Still Moving Media)

Place a ruler against the side of the face. If the ruler can touch the side of the face for less than 2.5cm, the face is round. This shape can wear a headdress of any shape but suits a halo.

High cheekbones with wider eyebrows and eyes. All these features mimic the shape of a heart. Leading ladies often have this face shape.

The cheekbones are level or central with the ears; the forehead is slimmer than the face at the eyes. Diamond shapes can have long necks.

| Square | Headband or bandeau |

| Pear | Halo (no diadem), curved |

| Oblong | Side tiara, suits all face shapes |

Place a ruler against the side of the face. If the ruler touches the side of the face for more than 3cm, the face may be square.

The jawline is angled outwards. The chin is wider and squarer than a round face. Pear-shaped faces tend to look good in period dramas. Helena Bonham Carter has a pear-shaped face.

Place a ruler against the side of the face If the ruler touches the side of the face for more than 5cm, the face may be oblong. Oblong-shaped faces, like the diamond, tend to have long necks.

Halo

*Suits round and
pear-shaped faces.*

With the shape of a halo as on a Madonna, this shape complements the roundness of the face. The Queen Mother always had tiaras of this shape. This style is featured in 'Isobel' in Chapter 5.

Diadem

Suits diamond and heart-shaped faces.

A tiara that has a pinnacle at the front. This style is featured in 'Lois' in Chapter 7.

Headband

Suits oblong and square-shaped faces.

This style forms a half-halo across the top of the head in line with the outer end of one eyebrow to the outer end of the other eyebrow; this is known as the vision line. This can be flat to head or raised up as a half-halo. Particularly suited to young girls and children, although recently there has been a trend for adults to wear this style of headdress with flowers on, known as the festival headdress. This style is featured in 'Megan' in Chapter 4, 'Faith' in Chapter 5 and 'Louise' in Chapter 6.

Apex shape

Suits heart and diamond-shaped faces.

An apex shape from outer eyebrow end to outer eyebrow end. The height is denoted by the measurement from eye to chin; the height of the apex should not exceed two thirds of this height. Some designers like to have one third of this height; it looks dainty and delicate. The height should ideally be between one and two thirds. This style is featured in 'Megan' in Chapter 4.

with permission of Annie Johnston

Gable shape

Suits diamond-shaped faces.

This shape originated in Tudor times, mimicking the shape of the gables on houses.

With permission Still Moving Media

Side tiara/headdress

Suits long square or oblong-shaped faces.

Positioned as a fascinator, this decoration is on the side and can either lie flat or stand up. The flatter shapes suit ladies with longer necks and the raised shapes suit ladies who have long square or oblong-shaped faces. This style is featured in 'Rachel' in Chapter 6 and 'Kathleen' in Chapter 7.

Circlet or forehead circlet

Suits round and pear-shaped faces.

Fits around the head. Not much height and quite thin. Usually made of chain or movable pieces in either stones or chain links. Suits round and pear-shaped faces where the face is wider at the cheekbones. This style is featured in 'India' in Chapter 9.

Back headdress

Suits all face shapes.

Taken from the back of the head measurement. Known in the millinery industry as the 'Jackie Kennedy'. Back-of-head position, great for low mantilla veils which are worn on the back of the head. This style is featured in 'Megan' in Chapter 4.

Hair clips/pins

Suit all face shapes

These can be placed in hairstyles like a chignon or bun. Usually worn at the back of the head. This style is featured in 'Lady Mary' in Chapter 8.

Hair vines

Suit all face shapes

Long ribbons of wire or cord, draped around the hair or intermingled with plaits or draped around hair buns and chignons. This style is featured in 'Polly' in Chapter 9.

Chapter 3
Basic Techniques

Within this Chapter I cover the very basics of making or covering a headband and how to affix headdresses to the head. Headdresses and hats are very much about engineering and making it stay on the head without the onlooker knowing how it's been done.

Every project within this book uses one or more of these basic techniques which show my ways of working. These techniques have been developed and tweaked over time. They work for me, and they work for many of my students, so it's worth taking some time to follow the instructions in this Chapter before embarking on the more detailed projects in the book.

Stitches

These are some of the stitches I use in this book's projects. They are familiar stitches; the only difference is you will be using wire instead of thread. These stitches were the basis of some of the stitches used within the medical industry, and they are still used today. The slip stitch known to milliners as the Jacob's ladder stitch is used in mending wounds in operations.

I use a Straw/milliners' needle size 6 and 0.2mm wire when sewing most of these stitches.

Preparation of sewing wire

To start, always thread a needle with no more than 60cm of wire, then double it on the needle so you are working with a 30cm length with a knot on the end (the knot can be easily hidden within the part you are sewing). It is better to work in short lengths because it stops the wire becoming entangled and kinking or folding.

Casting on a slipknot

Stitch through the knitted wire and pass the needle back through above your knot to anchor this first stitch.

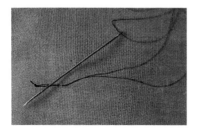
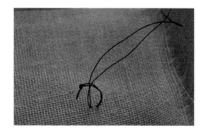

Casting off a slipknot

Make a stitch near the previous stitch you have made. Pull the wire through to make a loop, then slide the needle through the loop and pull tight until the loop is a knot.

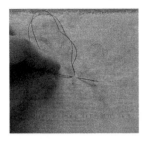 

Tying on a new thread of wire

Before you run out of wire, thread a new needle with another length of no more than 30cm of wire, double it on the needle so you are working with a 15cm length and knot the end.

Cast on your wire by making a stitch near the end of the previous wire (make sure that the last wire has not been cut off). Tie the old wire and the new wire tightly together, then cut off the old wire and begin sewing again with the new wire.

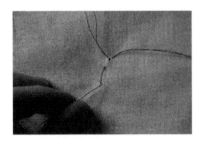 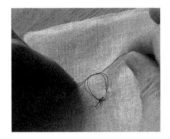

Types of stitch

Overstitch

A stitch made over an edge (Oxford Dictionaries).

Method: Cast on your wire and tuck the knot into the seam. Sew with close, diagonal stitches, bringing the needle over and over towards you. Take care not to take the stitches too deep or pull the wire too tight.

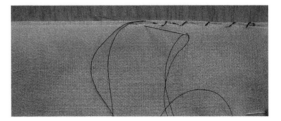

Slip stitch (Jacob's ladder)

A loose stitch joining layers of fabric and not visible externally (Oxford Dictionaries).

Method: Cast on your wire as above. Slip the needle through the fold of the knitted wire, then catch several threads off the bottom layer (directly underneath the top one), slip the needle back through the fold and repeat. This stitch is called the 'Jacob's ladder' stitch because of the ladder rungs it produces as you sew along the seam. Each stitch should be 0.5cm apart.

(Step 1)   (Step 2)

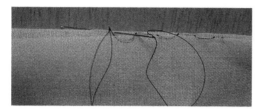

Stab stitch

A stitch in which the stitches on the visible surface are smaller than those underneath (Oxford Dictionaries).

Method: Cast on as above.

1. Push the needle from the wrong side of the fabric through to the right side of the fabric.
2. Push the needle from the right side of the fabric, roughly 1mm from where it came out, back to the wrong side. Move the needle to 2.5cm along and repeat.

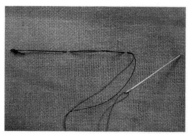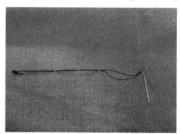

(Step 1)

(Step 2)

I am not going to do what other makers do when they say, 'I never use ready-made headbands.' There is a time and a place for all the different types of bands – some of our most famous milliners use ready-made bands, and I have no problem with that. It's when a milliner uses two headbands to anchor a heavy headdress that I do have a problem.

Philip Treacy, Stephen Jones and Bridget Bailey are masters of millinery; they understand the importance of the headband, its position and how to affix it to the head.

So here are my versions of headbands. You will be using both ready-made bands and ones you make yourself, and then you can choose what you want to use. Remember, it's all about the balance of the design and how it's placed on the band and then on the head.

When I worked with Suzanne Neville I always made my own headbands. I pioneered the technique outlined here, which is now followed by many other makers. This is a tried and tested method which I hope you will use too.

Materials needed

1.2mm wire   0.4mm wire

Tools needed

Ruler or tape measure   Flat back wire cutters   Round-nose pliers

Nylon jaw pliers   Craft scissors for wire

Beginner/intermediate level   Time taken: 30 mins

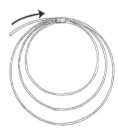

1. Undo your wires gradually. This will ensure that the wire doesn't coil up like a spring.

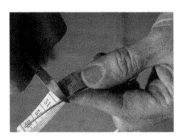
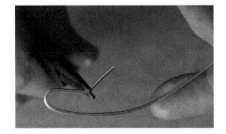

2. Cut off and discard any creased wire. Cut a length of 1.2mm base wire, 49cm long for an adult and 44cm long for a child (this is a standard length for an average 57cm circlet), and two lengths of 0.4mm wrapping wire 60cm long. On the tiara headband wire, measure 2.5cm in from each end and mark by rubbing the round-nose pliers around the 1.2mm base wire bar.

3. Using the round-nose pliers, bend the wire over at the marks, then bend the wire ends back to form a crook so they sit close to the main 1.2mm base wire bar and form a loop at each end (to attach the tiara to the hair with grips or elastic).
4. From the folded ends, measure 5cm along the bar; mark this and the central position by rubbing the round-nose pliers gently around the base wire bar.

Forming ends of base wire bar

1. Fold one piece of the 0.4mm wire in half gently, but do not crease. Slip the loop of fine wire over the end of the base wire bar.

2. Wrap the 0.4mm fine wire round the loop on the main bar to bind the ends neatly together, until the cut end of the base wire is neatly covered. Continue wrapping the wire up to the 5cm mark on the base wire bar.

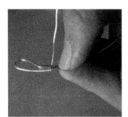 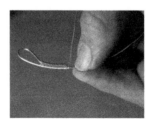 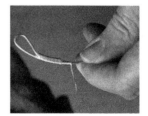

3. Cut the wire off close to the base wire bar and round off the cut ends using nylon jaw pliers.

 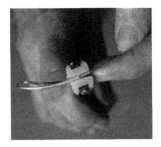

4. Repeat with remaining length of wrapping wire at the opposite end of tiara. Bend the base wire bar into a curve to fit head.

A tip for bending the bar to head shape: bounce the wire in between your hands, curving the base wire bar gently. The base wire bar will not curve back to the original spring, as it has been handled and straightened.

Covering a headband with knitted wire

These headbands can be used for all headband-mounted headdresses. The tubular wire helps the headband to cling tighter to the head and not slip in the hair. It also makes the headband easier to sew on than a satin-covered headband.

Materials needed

Ready-made headband   15mm wide 0.1mm tight knit wire (tubular)

0.2mm silver-plated non-tarnish wire   All-purpose glue

Tools needed

Ruler or tape measure   Pencil   Craft scissors

Straw/milliners' needle, size 6   Nylon jaw pliers

Beginner/intermediate level   Time taken: 20 mins

1. Take a ready-made headband; ease the headband open slightly by pulling both sides apart. Bending the band in this way stretches the size of the headband.

2. Measure a 38cm piece of 15mm wide 0.1mm tight knit wire (your headband should measure about 39cm; you will need to make the knitted wire 1cm shorter so you can stretch to the correct length). Hold each end of the knitted wire and pull until it will stretch no more.

3. Open the knitted tube with a pencil, then slide the headband inside the tube; you will have excess tubing. Divide this excess to either end.

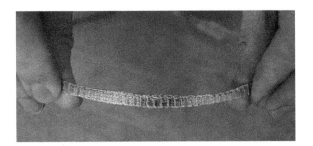

4. Twist the excess once on one end of the band. Roll the knitted wire to tighten it to your band. Work your way along the band to the other end, making sure the knitted wire is lying smooth and level, then twist the excess once more at the other end.

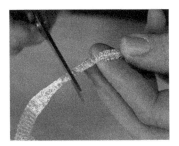

5. Trim the excess knitted wire down to 1cm at each end. Tuck this excess under, towards the inside of the band. Thread a needle with no more than 60cm of 0.2mm wire, double it on the needle so you are working with a 30cm length with a knot on the end.

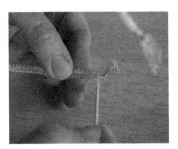

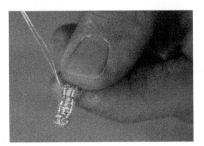

6. Cast on the wire, hiding the knot under the fold, and apply a small amount of all-purpose glue under the fold. Wait until tacky, then bind by wrapping the wire around and around the end of the band neatly. Repeat on the other side.

7. Cast off the wire using a slipknot, slide the needle under the bound wire and cut off the excess wire, repeat on the other side. Smooth and squash each end using nylon jaw pliers. Just to make sure all wires do not come undone I put a dab of glue on each end of the headband.

Making a simple wire base

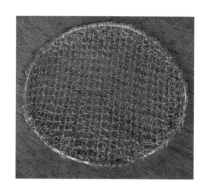

Headdresses without bases tend to slip and slide across the hair. Making your own bases using coarse knitted wire gets rid of this problem. You can use tight knitted wire to make linings.

Materials needed

0.8mm wire for frame

0.2mm wire for sewing

0.4mm wire for binding

85mm wide 0.2mm coarse knitted wire

Tools needed

Ruler or tape measure

Straw/milliners' needle, size 6

Flat-back wire cutters

Craft scissors

Nylon jaw pliers

Beginner/intermediate level   *Time taken: 1 hour*

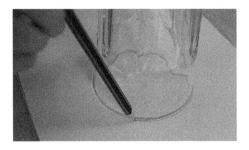

1. Cut the 0.8mm wire the length of the shape you wish to make, allowing a 2.5cm overlap.

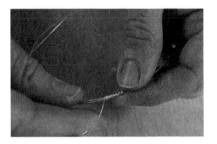

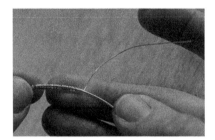

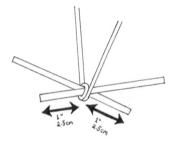

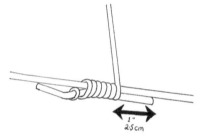

2. Take a 60cm length of 0.4mm wire and fold it in half. Hook on in the centre of the join and bind the wires, as you did when making Denise's handmade tiara headband earlier in this Chapter, closing the gap and working to one end. Overlap 1cm onto the base wire to make the ends safe. This also stops the wire from moving.

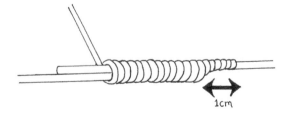

3. Gently separate the base wires and thread through a new 60cm length of 0.4mm wire, folded in half, to bind in the opposite direction. This will anchor the binding wire and stop it slipping apart. Overlap 1cm onto the base wire again to make the ends safe and stop the base wires from moving.

4. Cut the 0.4mm wire close to the bar with flat-back wire cutters.

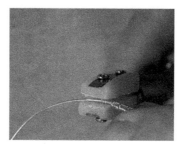

5. Smooth off the cut end with nylon jaw pliers.

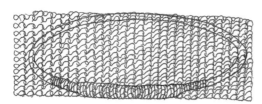 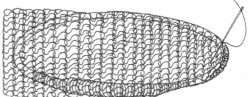

6. Slide the frame into the tube of knitted wire. Fold in any raw edges, then overstitch using a Straw/milliners' needle threaded with 0.2mm wire around the frame.

 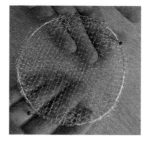 

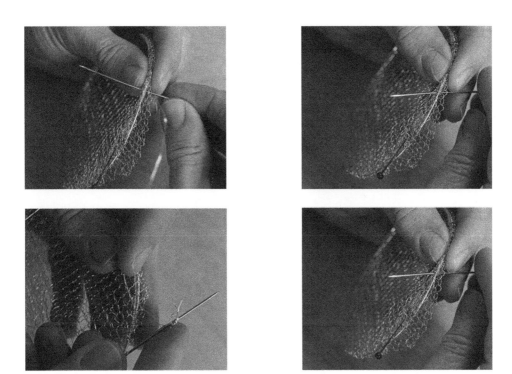

This base has also been marked into quarters using 0.2mm wire stitches; this is helpful when positioning stones etc.

'Grip wire' is a term I use to define a piece of wire used to provide a place to attach clips when fixing into hair.

Materials needed

1.0mm wire for a strong hold; otherwise use 0.8mm or 0.6mm wire. In this project, I am using 1.0mm wire.

0.2mm wire for stitching in place

Tools needed

Nylon jaw pliers   Tape measure

Flat-back wire cutters   Straw/ milliners' needles, size 6

Beginner/intermediate level   Time taken: 10 mins

The grip wire will usually be towards the top of your piece, above the comb.

1. Make a small loop at the end of the 1.0mm wire using round-nose pliers, wrapping the wire around one of the round prongs of the pliers.

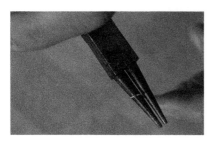
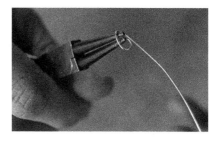

2. Place the 1.0mm wire onto the piece and measure the required length. In this case the back of the finished piece measured 10cm, so I used a 15cm length of wire. This allowed 2.5cm each end of the grip wire to create a loop.

3. Flatten the cut ends of each loop using nylon jaw pliers.
4. Stitch through the loop using 0.2mm wire to attach the grip wire to your piece.

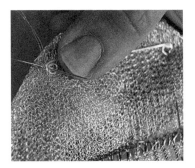

Creating a design guide

This is a trick I picked up when working in costume hire companies. One of the ways of tracking jewellery, eyeglasses and other small items was to photocopy them. This was great for checking pieces in and out of shipping containers.

You can use this technique in your designing. When you don't know how to place your metal plate pieces in your design, this tip will help you to plan and record your design.

Materials needed

A sheet of acetate   Double-sided sticky tape

Tools needed

Poly pocket plastic file   Photocopier/printer-scanner

1. Take a sheet of clear acetate film. Stick on strips of double-sided tape; these can be made as wide or as deep as you want. Number the tape strips so you can replace them when you have finished using the sheet.

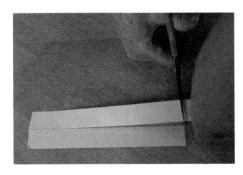
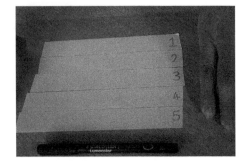

2. Arrange the pieces on the tape to form your design.

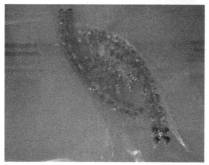

3. Slide into a poly pocket plastic file to protect the glass of your photocopier. Photocopy front and back.

This photocopy can be used as a guide to measure the wire for your tiara frame. It can also be referred to as you are making your tiara, and will be useful should you ever need to repeat a design. I use this method all the time

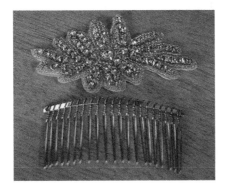

The amount, or size, of decoration you can add to a comb is restricted by the depth of the comb teeth. Many of my students want to add more trimmings than a standard comb will take. The answer is to extend the comb.

I have used this method many times when making headdresses for brides who want either fresh or handmade silk flowers on a small comb. Again, I owe this technique to the knitted wire. I hope this helps with bulky decorations.

Materials needed

0.8mm wire for frame   0.4mm wire for binding   0.2mm wire for sewing

15mm wide 0.1mm tight knitted wire   Metal comb

Tools needed

Ruler or tape measure   Flat-back wire cutters   Nylon jaw pliers

Beginner/intermediate level   Time taken: 1 hour

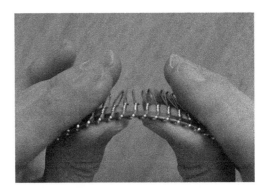

Before you begin, take your comb and arch it by putting pressure on the bar with your thumbs.

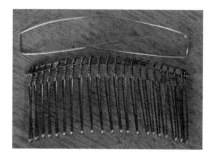
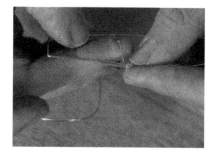

1. Measure the 0.8mm wire to fit the bar end of the comb and make an outline around the shape needed with a 7.5cm overlap. Join the wire by binding with 0.4mm wire as shown in 'Making simple wire bases', above. Smooth off the cut ends with nylon jaw pliers. The 0.8mm wire will allow you to bend and shape your piece.

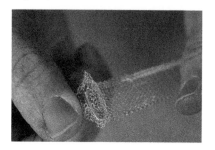
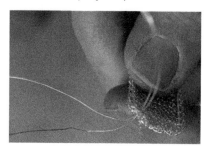

2. Cover the wire outline with 15mm wide 0.1mm tight knit wire. Turn the open ends of the knitted wire tube inside the tube for a safe, neat finish.

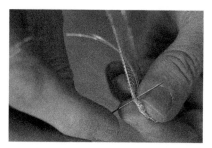

3. Using an overstitch, sew the frame to the knitted wire with 0.2mm wire.

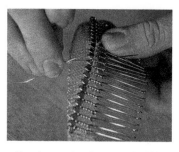
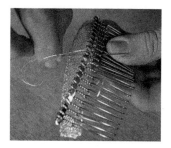

4. Sew the frame to the comb. Place the frame to fit on the underside of the bar. Overstitch the base to the comb bar with 0.2mm wire. It is easier to locate the centre of the comb bar and the frame first.

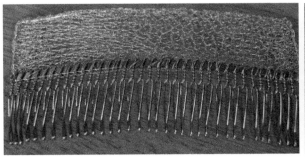 

5. Add the decoration to the bar.

Attaching the comb

There are many ways to attach a comb. I have even seen a plastic comb glued to a headdress. Not a brilliant idea as it does not stay put. I use metal combs as they are the ones with the most grip, and they are sturdy and easy to sew.

Materials needed

0.2mm wire   Metal comb

Tools needed

Straw/milliners' needle, size 0.6   Craft scissors/wire cutters

Beginner/intermediate level   Time taken: 30 mins

1. Place the comb on the frame with the convex side on the inside of the frame. This is so the concave side of the comb is ready to meet the curve on the head when sewn.
2. Thread a needle with no more than 60cm of 0.2mm wire, double it on the needle so you are working with a 30cm length and knot the end.

3. Starting from the centre of the comb and working your way outwards, overstitch the comb to the lined frame. Repeat from the centre to the other end using the same stitch.

Ribbon loops

Ribbon loops are a simple yet effective way of attaching a tiara to the head without fastenings being visible. They can be added to a framed tiara piece or used on wire headdress cages.

Materials needed

15mm wide 0.1mm tight knit wire   2 x 1.25mm copper jump rings

0.2mm wire for sewing   1m of 0.5mm ribbon

Tools needed

Craft scissors   Straw/milliners' needle, size 6

Beginner/intermediate level   *Time taken: 30 mins*

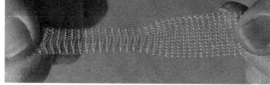

1. Take a length of 15mm wide 0.1mm tight knit wire. Stretch and cut to required lengths. I used 4cm on each loop.

2. Thread through the 1.25mm copper jump rings. Fold halfway.
3. Stitch into your piece using 0.2mm wire.

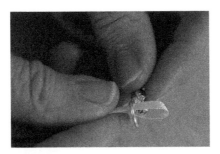

4. Take a 50cm length of 0.5mm wide ribbon. Cut the ends to form points diagonally.

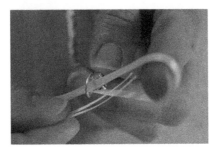

5. Double and thread through the loop.

6. Match up the ends, then thread back through the ribbon loop itself.

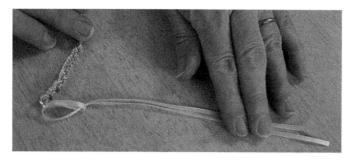 

7. Pull the ribbon through the loop and tighten.

This is a very old-fashioned way of attaching stones to garments. The reason for my use of it is that wires can be passed through the backs of the stones so they can be suspended in mid-air. Here's how you attach the clasps.

Some diamante stones come in two parts that need assembling before use: the flat-back stones and the metal sew-on back claw settings.

Materials needed

Swarovski foiled flat-backed crystals   Metal sew-on back settings or clasps

In this case, I am using size SS40 with the corresponding setting.

Tools needed

Stone-setting tool

Beginner/intermediate level   Time taken: 10 mins

Make sure your crystals and stone settings are the correct size. Most stones are sold with matching clasps advised by the company. I purchased mine from Creative Beadcraft.

1. Place the stone inside the clasp, crystal side up, foiled back closest to the clasp.

2. Push down with the stone-setting tool until all the clasps are holding the stone.

3. With some of the clasps there is a point where you can hear the stone touch the underside of the tool; that's when you should stop pushing.

If one of the clasp hooks does not look as if it is gripping the stone, you can always use the nylon jaw pliers to squeeze it into place.

Chapter 4
Beaded Tiaras

The first tiara I made was for the wedding dress designer Suzanne Neville in the 1990s; it was a threaded-through beaded piece. It was featured on the front cover of a magazine and my career in tiara-making took off.

When I look back at my early pieces I cringe! I would never make them in that way now, and yet my journey from that first piece has taught me much over the years. No one ever showed me how to make a tiara; likewise, no one taught me what the wires did or how to use them to incorporate beads into the headbands. That was a long personal study with a lap-tray of beads and all the wires, practising, practising and practising. Soon my tiaras were in high demand by magazines and designers alike. So clearly practice does make perfect.

To get you started I've included two foundation pieces from which you can develop as your skills improve and alter with changing fashions.

Wire and beads (beaded tiara methods)

Twisted pearl

This is a popular method in tiara-making as it minimises the weight of the finished piece. This method is used in 'Megan' later in this Chapter.

Four-wire threaded

This is a design that can be used either horizontally or vertically. By threading beads across four wires, it is ideal for filling space in tiara designs. You can use most sizes and types of beads to give a range of effects. This method is used in 'Jessica' later in this Chapter.

This twisted pearl piece can be worn as either a tiara or a decoration at the back of the head as shown in the photograph.

Materials needed

One of Denise's handmade tiara headbands (see Chapter 3)

0.4mm wire for wrapping and twisting

30 beads (e.g. pearls) in two sizes; I have used 7mm and 5mm pearls

15mm 0.1 tight knit wire for covering (optional)

Tools needed

Tape measure   Flat-back wire cutters   Craft scissors   Nylon jaw pliers

Beginner level   *Time taken: 2 hours*

Make the tiara headband (using 1.2mm base wire) as described in Chapter 3.

Make twisted stems

1. From the 0.4mm wire, cut 20 pieces 20cm long and 10 pieces 15cm long. Thread a large bead on to each long length and a small one on to the shorter lengths, placing them halfway along each wire.

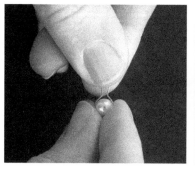  

2. Working with one length at a time, hold both ends of the wire open with one hand and the bead in the other. The hand holding the bead does the turning. Keeping the bead central, start twisting the wires together, turning the bead away from you and keeping the ends of the wire open in the other hand. Do not change the position of the other hand as you will alter the flow of the twist.

3. Twist the wire until you get to about 4cm away from the ends, leaving the ends loose for attaching to the tiara base.

4. Twist the remaining beaded wires in this way, making the twisted sections slightly different in length; the difference can be as much as 3cm and as little as 1cm.

Attach stems

1. Working outwards from the central mark on the tiara base, start to position your twisted beads, wrapping the loose ends of the wires around the tiara base wire, with at least five twists each side of the stem. Note that all stems should be wrapped onto the band facing the same way – there is a front and a back, so take care to join each stem the same way, as shown in the photographs. Position larger beads in the centre and smaller ones at the sides and use the longer beaded wires near the centre to form an apex.

 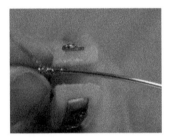

2. When you decide that your tiara is at the desired size and height, wind any excess wire around the base. Smooth out with nylon jaw pliers, being careful not to break any of the wires.

Finishing

 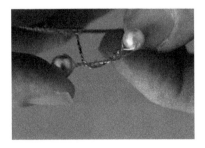

1. To stop the tiara from drooping, loop the wire stems together, rather like the first stage of tying a shoelace. To create a more stable structure, loosely tie each wire stem to the next working from the centre outwards.

2. If you want to tidy up your wires where they join the band you can cover them with 15mm 0.1 tight knitted wire (as shown in the next project, 'Jessica'). Please make sure that all your wires are safe and have been rounded off with nylon jaw pliers. It is the maker's responsibility to make all products safe to wear.

Becky is a first-time student; she has had one lesson with me and is a complete novice with using any form of wire. She is a felt maker.

Becky said:

I loved winding the pearls and would definitely make this again and use this technique on other designs.

I found attaching the twisted stems quite fiddly as they kept slipping around the base.

Denise's answer:

You could try gluing a piece of knitted wire to the bar first. Take a look at 'Jessica' [below], which uses this technique, steps 2–4.

Jessica (threaded through weaving)

Here is one of the most versatile techniques that I have used in tiara-making. It looks fresh, is simple to use and can make both horizontal and vertical pieces.

Materials needed

One of Denise's handmade tiara headbands (see Chapter 3), made but unbound at one of the ends.

15mm wide 0.1mm tight knit wire (tubular)

0.2mm wire for binding and stitching

All-purpose glue

0.4mm wire for threading

Bicone iridescent (AB) crystals (I used sizes 4mm and 6mm)

3mm bullion wire (silver-plated)

Tools needed

Ruler or tape measure   Craft scissors

Nylon jaw pliers   Straw/milliners' needle, size 6

Intermediate level   *Time taken: 2 hours*

Preparing the headband

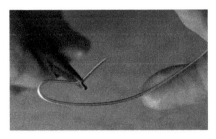

1. Make up a tiara headband as described in Chapter 3. Bend the wire but do not bind one of the ends.

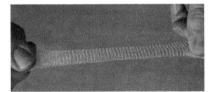  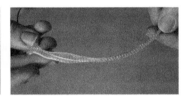

One of the problems with metal headbands is that decoration tends to slip. Fixing a length of knitted wire to the headband can solve this problem.

2. Take a 10cm strip of 15mm wide 0.1mm tight knit wire tube, stretch as shown and thread over the headband. Stretch out the knitted wire and roll it between your fingers until it is tight against the headband. Slide the knitted wire along the headband until only 6.5 cm of the unbound end of the headband is visible.
3. Take two lengths (approx. 25cm each) of 0.2mm wire and bind each end of the knitted wire to anchor it to the headband.

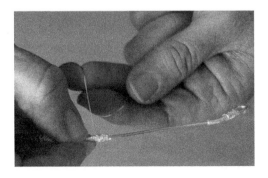

4. Glue the two ends in place with a blob of all-purpose glue.

Making the beaded pieces

Make up the beaded pieces in graduated finished lengths of between 6cm and 12cm.1.

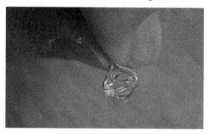

1. Take two lengths of 0.4mm wire, each 32cm long. Thread both wires through a 4mm crystal until the crystal sits in the middle of the wire length. Bend the wires around the crystal and pinch them.

2. Split the wires into three and one. Thread the three wire ends through a second 4mm crystal and slide the crystal down the wires until it sits next to the first crystal. Smooth the single wire end around the outside of the second crystal. Pinch all four wire ends together at the bottom of the second crystal. (**Tip:** If you are having difficulty with the bore holes on the small beads, replace one length of 0.4mm wire with 0.2mm wire, but keep the 0.2mm wire running through the centre of the beads and use the 0.4mm wire to smooth around the outside.)

3. Repeat step 2 by splitting the wires into three and one again, using a different wire to smooth round the crystal each time. You can vary the sizes of the crystals to create different effects, but be aware that too many large crystals or glass beads will make your headdress heavy.

 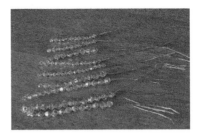

4. Continue until the desired length is achieved. You can gradually increase the size of the crystals along the length, or use smaller crystals on the shorter lengths and larger crystals on the longer ones. You will need to leave at least 8cm of wire at the bottom of the threaded length to attach to the headband. I made three 6cm lengths, three 9cm lengths and three 12cm lengths.

Making the bullion pieces

1. Cut the bullion into different lengths: two 6cm, two 8cm, two 10cm.
2. Cut one 30cm piece of 0.4mm wire.

 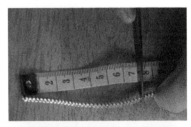

 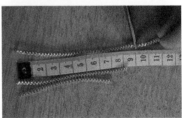

3. Thread the 0.4mm wire through a 4mm crystal until the crystal sits in the middle of the wire length.
4. Fold the wire around the crystal so that the two ends of the wire meet.
5. Thread the bullion onto both ends of the wire. (**Tip**: Keep turning the wires as you pull the bullion over them to avoid the wires coming out midway through the bullion.)

6. Spread the wire ends to push the bullion up tight under the crystal.

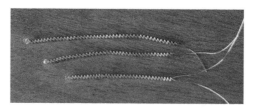

7. Repeat steps 2 to 6 until you have enough bullion pieces for your design. (**Tip**: Less is more.)

Attaching stems

1. Working along the knitted wire on the tiara base, position your crystal stems and bullion stems at random, mixing lengths. Wrap the loose wire at the bottom of each stem around the tiara base; wrap only a couple of times initially so you can reposition if necessary.
2. When you have the desired effect, wind off the remaining wire as neatly as possible around the base.
3. Cut off any excess stem wire and smooth out with nylon jaw pliers. Be careful not to break any of the wires during the smoothing process.

Finishing

1. Take another length of 15mm wide 0.1mm tight knit wire, long enough to cover the twisted wires.
2. Fold the 15mm wide 0.1mm tight knit wire in half, with the ends above the band.
3. Stretch and roll the knitted wire onto the band at each end.

4. Sew the open edges of the knitted wire together with 0.2mm wire to hold the stems upright.
5. Bind the ends with 0.2mm wire and glue the two ends in place with a blob of all-purpose glue.
6. Don't forget to finish the ends of your headband by wrapping as described in 'Denise's handmade tiara headband' in Chapter 3.

Once you have mastered the basic techniques you can experiment with different styles. This picture shows one of my halo tiaras using the techniques for making up the beaded pieces used in this project. Pearls are used rather than crystals and the beadwork goes from side to side instead of top to bottom.

Chapter 5

Using Stones with Wire

Making a tiara look delicate and dainty is a very hard task.

Many tiara makers make the mistake of believing they can charge more if they chuck everything they can at it. This never works. My students know my mantra is 'Less is more'.

The best designers know how to use embellishments for best effect. There is elegance in simplicity, exemplified by the likes of Audrey Hepburn. While working through this Chapter, keep my mantra in mind. Less is more. I promise you will be amazed at the results, and your pieces can look like they walked off a page of *Brides Magazine*.

The following two projects were found by experimenting with backed stones and wires. The 'Faith' tiara was also made for Suzanne Neville in 1993 and I liked it so much I remade it for my daughters to wear at my own wedding in 2012.

I have included two projects that use this method: one with acrylic stones (halo shape), and the other with Swarovski stones (headband shape).

The acrylic stones I use already have the backs attached, which makes them easy to use, and they look very effective. Swarovski stones, which you are more likely to see sewn on to fabric, do not come ready-backed, so you need to attach the sew-on backs with a clamping tool.

This introductory-level project uses acrylic stones with the backs already attached.

Materials needed

One of Denise's handmade tiara headbands (see Chapter 3)

0.8mm wire for threading

Acrylic stones with mounts (I used three 18mm x 25mm octagonal PES50 and four 8.5mm round PES52 from Creative Beadcraft)

0.4mm wire for binding

Tools needed

Tape measure	Flat-back wire cutters	Round-nose pliers
Craft scissors	Red felt tip pen	Nylon jaw pliers

Beginner/intermediate level   Time taken: 2 hours

1. Make the headband as described in 'Denise's handmade tiara headband' in Chapter 3.

2. Cut two 45cm lengths of 0.8mm wire and mark the centre of each length by gently rolling round-nose pliers around the wire.

3. Decide which order you want to place your stones before you place them onto the headband. Always design your tiara with a large central stone.

4. Thread each wire through the central stone. Line the stone up in the centre of the wires. (**Tip:** You can trim the ends of the wires if necessary and loosen the mount slightly to ease threading, then retighten when in position.)

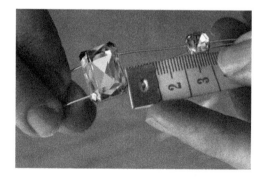

5. Thread the stones on either side of the central stone in your design (step 3) onto the wire.

6. Push the stones added in step 5 towards the central stone, ensuring they are equidistant on both sides, with approximately 2.5cm between each stone.

7. Repeat steps 5 and 6 as per your own design. Make sure the distances between each stone are the same, otherwise your finished piece will look lopsided.

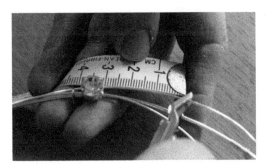

8. Cut the 0.8mm wire at the top of your design, leaving 3cm from the end of your outermost stone.

9. Cut the 0.8mm wire at the bottom of your design, leaving 3.5cm from the end of your outermost stone. (**Tip**: Cutting the two wires at different lengths makes your final piece look neater.)

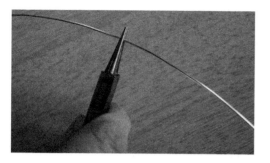

10. Take your headband and measure the outside edge to find the centre of the headband.
11. Mark the centre by rubbing the round-nose pliers on the bar. I find a red pen helps to show the mark.

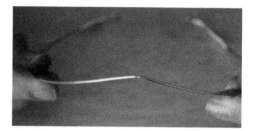

12. Holding the underside of your headband at the centre mark, gently push outwards to make a slight fold in the headband. **Tip**:This technique was first used by the Victorians to raise the bar of the headband above the hair and continues to be used to this day for royal tiaras.
13. Cut three 28cm lengths of 0.4mm wire (one for each large stone).

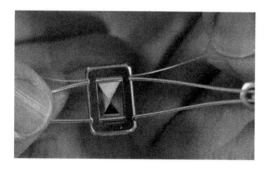

14. Thread a length of the 0.4mm wire through the lower holes at either side of the central stone (the wire needs to go into through the lower hole on one side of the stone and out of the lower hole on the other side).
15. Repeat step 14 for each large stone.

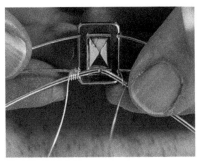

16. Align the central stone with the centre of the headband.

17. Bind the 0.8mm wire to the headband by using the 0.4mm wire you have just threaded through the large stones. Start by securing the central stone and the 0.8mm wire frame to the headband and repeat until you have secured all large stones in this way. Make sure the stones are still equidistant.

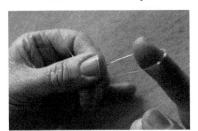  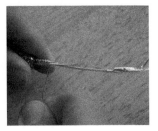

18. Cut off any excess wire and round off using nylon jaw pliers to remove any sharp ends.

Tip: You can mark the headband (with the round-nosed pliers) if it helps you to keep all the stones in place.

To finish the headband

1. Rest the remaining 0.8mm wire on top of the headband using a 60cm length of 0.4mm wire folded in the middle.
2. Hook the folded end of the wire onto the headband on the outside of the outermost stone and start binding from the stone towards the cut ends of the 0.8mm wire. When you reach the cut end, continue binding onto the headband 1cm beyond the cut end or to meet the binding from the end of the headband.

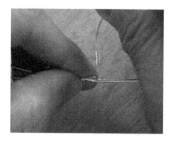 

3. Repeat steps 1 and 2 on the other side of the headband.
4. When you have finished, you may need to gently manipulate the headband to fit the shape of the head.

Nicky tested this project; she is a junior school art teacher. She had never used wire before, so she did not know what to expect.

Nicky said:

After making the Isobel headband it inspired me to look at designs on the internet and gave me the confidence to have a go at my own design. I am really pleased with the results and have had lots of compliments from my friends.

Nicky's Tiara

Nicky, inspired by the test piece, bought some similar stones and made a tiara for herself:

Nicky asked:

> When using the halo style to make my own design I found that the stones were still able to move about after wiring them. How could I stop this?

Denise's answer:

> If you use larger stones they can be too heavy, so you also need to wire the tops of the stones to support the headband and keep them in place.

Introduction to Swarovski stones

Swarovski stones are a quality alternative to diamonds and I am a great advocate. You can make cheap paste stones look fabulous by adding one or two of these more expensive stones and make a cheaper tiara look incredible. The addition of just one Swarovski, which sets off the stones on either side, brings the piece alive.

You can make diamante pieces glisten more by using an eight-facet cut stone to reflect light that will bounce off the other stones.

The following project (Faith) uses Swarovski crystals more usually seen sewn on to fabric. Glass stones can be bought with the backs attached from EIMASS in Burnham, but the Swarovski crystals will require sew-on settings to be attached using a stone-setting tool, all available from Creative Beadcraft.

I used to make this design a lot for Suzanne Neville. It is fiddly but doesn't need much equipment.

With permission of Helen Lee

Isobel, Faith and Megan at the author's wedding in 2012

The method explained here is a favourite of mine and this was one of my first pieces to be featured in *Brides Magazine*. This is the headdress my daughters wore for my wedding, barely noticing they had it on all day as it is such a light and delicate piece. I hope you enjoy this piece as much as I have!

Materials needed

One of Denise's handmade tiara headbands (Chapter 3)

Swarovski Xilion Rose crystals (I used seven SS48 and four SS30 from Creative Beadcraft)

Sew-on settings to match the stones

0.6mm wire for threading

0.4mm wire for binding

Tools needed

Small piece of compressed foam to press the stone-setting tool against

Stone-setting tool   Tape measure   Flat-back wire cutters

Round-nose pliers   Nylon jaw pliers

Advanced level   *Time taken: 2 hours*

1. Make the headband as described in 'Denise's handmade tiara headband' in Chapter 3.

2. This design requires flat-backed stones to be attached to sew-on settings in order for the wires to cross over smoothly. Place the stone centrally in the sew-on setting. (**Tip:** Use a piece of compressed foam to press into as you set the stones; this will hold the stone and the clamp together, give a smoother press and prevent the stones cracking if you push too quickly.)

 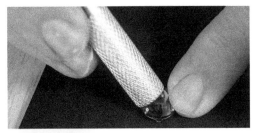

3. Using the largest end of the stone-setting tool, loosely set the stones into the sew-on settings.

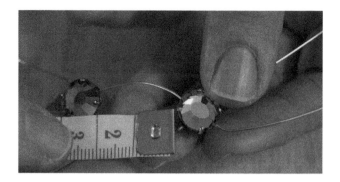

4. Measure and cut two 70cm lengths of 0.6mm wire. (**Tip:** Always work carefully to avoid kinks in the wire.)

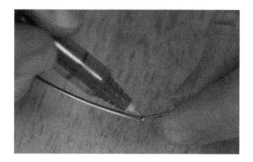

5. Take a stone and thread both wires through it until the stone sits halfway along the wires. Take care not to scratch the backs of the stones while threading. (**Tip:** Sometimes you will need to release the stones slightly in the settings to allow the wires to pass through, but be careful not to loosen too much or the stones will fall out.)

6. Repeat with the next stone on each side, checking the wires do not kink and the stones are the correct way up. Measure carefully to ensure all stones are equidistant, 2.5cm apart for an adult, 2cm apart for a child.

7. When each stone is in position, tighten the settings using the round-nose pliers, making sure the wires pass through the channels on the setting.

8. Keep alternating sides until all the large stones are attached. You should be left with about 7cm of wire each end.

9. Finish each side with two smaller stones.

Finishing on the headband

1. Take your headband and measure the outside edge to find the centre of the headband.
2. Mark the centre by rubbing the round-nose pliers on the bar. I find a red pen helps to show the mark.
3. Take 20cm of 0.4mm wire and thread through one of the wire channels on the centre stone alongside the 0.6mm wire. (**Tip**: As more wire goes through the stone there is a danger of the stone popping out of its setting, so hold the stone in position between your finger and thumb to prevent this.)
4. Align the centre stone with the centre mark.
5. Wrap one wire around the headband to secure the stone in one direction. Repeat the other side, wrapping in the opposite direction.
6. Check position, then continue to wrap approximately five times each side. Squeeze the binding to tighten and keep it hidden behind the stone. Trim off excess.
7. Repeat for each stone, alternating sides and checking position of the centre stone each time to avoid slippage.

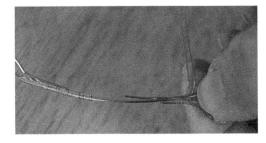 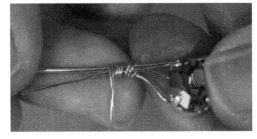

Finishing the cut ends of the wire

1. Rest the remaining 0.8mm wire on top of the headband using a 60cm length of 0.4mm wire doubled as you did with 'Isobel' (under 'To finish the headband').
2. Hook the folded end onto the headband and start binding from the stone towards the cut ends of the 0.8mm wire. When you reach the end, continue binding onto the headband 1cm over the cut end or to meet the binding from the end of the headband.
3. Repeat on the other side.
4. When you have finished, some headbands need shaping to fit the head.

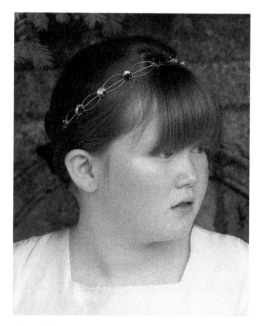

Cery in Blue and Silver version of 'Faith Headband'

Chapter 6

Making Wired Fabric from Scratch

The first time I made my own wired fabric, I was not impressed. I like tiaras to be tidy, and the thought of messy wire that looked like scribbles made me feel a little uneasy. But, fortunately, I got over my reservations and I now love it! Scrunching wire to make fabric is not new; it has been done since medieval times when they wove fresh flowers between the wires.

I made a tiara using wired fabric for a children's fairy costumes article for *Essentials* magazine (Christmas issue, December 2000 and January 2001). I used it again in 2004 for my niece's wedding headdress, but this time it was edged in wire: a small coronet with stones threaded through the wire.

In 2009 I took some students to New York on a field trip. An exhibition of the work of sculptor Alexander Calder at the Metropolitan Museum of Art mesmerised me. I realised there and then that I needed to release my inner designer again and get back to making tiaras.

By this time, I discovered that you could get finer and more delicate wires. No longer are the wires crude and thick – you can now get them in any size and many colours.

The next two projects show you how to create fabric from wire and back any pieces that you want to make into headdresses.

With permission of Cotswold Style and Still Moving Media

This project makes an ideal accessory for a child. It is a simple design which is lightweight and easy to wear

Materials needed

One of Denise's handmade tiara headbands (see Chapter 3). This needs to be made from 1.0mm wire as you need a lighter weight for a child.

35m spool of 0.3mm or 0.4mm wire. You will use approximately 20m.

0.2mm wire for sewing.

A selection of beads, in various sizes and coordinating colours. I used approximately 40 AB bicone stones in cerise, a mixture of 4mm and 6mm.

Tools needed

Flat-back wire cutters   Craft scissors   Tape measure

Round-nose pliers Long glass-headed pins Straw/milliners' needles

Beginner level   Time taken: 2 hours

1.0mm wire is a soft wire suitable for a child's headband. I also recommend using 0.3mm wire for scrunching on a child's headdress, as it is relatively flexible and creates a soft texture in the finished piece.

 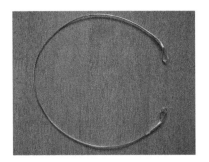

1. Make a headband as described in 'Denise's handmade tiara headband', Chapter 3.

 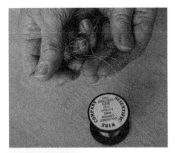

2. Unravel 0.3mm wire from the reel, gathering and loosely scrunching the wire as you go. (**Tip:** Try to keep the end visible or you may take some time trying to find it again at the end (as I did!))

Keep working like this until you have a piece that is roughly 7cm wide and the same length as your headband. To achieve this, you will need to scrunch approximately 20m of the wire.

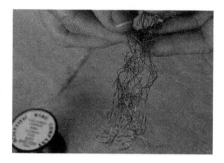

3. Unroll a further 2m of wire and, using the cut end, start sewing the scrunched wire together by loosely threading in and out.

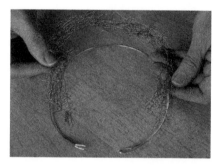

4. Manipulate the scrunched wire to make it the same length as your headband.

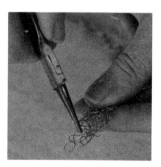 

5. Take the cut ends and, using a pair of round-nose pliers, roll the ends to hide them in the scrunched wire and make them safe.

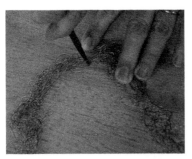

6. Take the round-nose pliers and begin twisting the wires into tighter curls, gradually reducing the width of the scrunched wire as it becomes more densely twisted. The length of the scrunched wire must stay the same as that of the headband. Where wires are loosely scrunched at the edges, use the round-nose pliers to twist them together and push them into the scrunched wire.

7. Continue to pull, twist and scrunch the wire, looking out for any areas that need extra work, as you create your own freestyle. Work until you have a densely scrunched band the same length as your headband. Using the long glass-headed pins, pin the scrunched wire to the headband.

8. You are now ready to decorate the band. Thread a needle with a 60cm length of 0.2mm wire, double it on the needle so you are working with a final length of 30cm and knot the end. Use long Straw/milliners' needles; 7s for bead threading and 8s and 9s for thicker wire are most useful. (**Tip:** You will need to use separate needles for fabric sewing and wire work as the metal wire will quickly blunt your needles.)

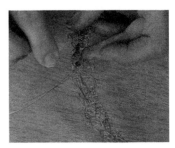

9. Find the centre of the scrunched band and insert a pin to mark it.

10. Divide the beads into two equal quantities – one for each side of the pin – and start sewing on your beads. You should be able to sew through each bead twice. Weave the wire through the headband to where you want to position the next bead and repeat, scattering the beads across the headband. You can add as many beads as you want to create your own design.

11. Using the 0.2mm wire, sew through the scrunched wire, anchoring it to the loop of the headband. Continue securing the scrunched wire to the headband using the 0.2mm wire; secure the scrunched wire by overstitching as you work along the headband. (Tip: You may need to overstitch twice in the same place to make sure it is properly secured.) Each overstitch should be approximately 1cm apart.

Irene Spencer, a mother and grandmother who does some craft but has never worked in wire before, made this piece.

Irene said:

The instructions were easy when I started to make it, but just reading them in advance made me think it was going to be too difficult.

Irene asked:

The most difficult part was attaching to the headband as I was pushing the scrunched wire about too much. Will I make the tiara look different to what you have made?

Denise's answer:

The great thing about this kind of design and fabric is that each piece is individual. Nothing you do is wrong and this type of designing is unique to the tiara industry. I think the tiara you have made is beautiful and your granddaughter, as we see here, is very comfortable wearing it:

Jessica wearing Irene's headband

In these pictures the headdresses has been made using the same techniques in various ways.

Rachel (teardrop-shaped headpiece)

This is a sample that I made for *Cotswold Style* magazine. I also made a variation of this style for Paloma Faith and for my own wedding headdress. It has been tried and tested on real people. Enjoy!

Materials needed

Paper and pen/pencil for template

1.0mm wire for base

0.4mm wire for binding

0.2mm wire for scrunching and stitching

Feathers (I used emu, although biot, ostrich or aigrette would also be suitable)

A selection of beads, in various sizes and coordinating colours (I used 4mm crystal bicones and 2mm metal beads)

85mm wide 0.1mm tight knit wire for lining

Tools needed

Flat-back wire cutters	Nylon jaw pliers	Round-nose pliers
Craft scissors	Tape measure	Straw/milliners' needle, size 6

Advanced level   *Time taken: 3 hours*

Making the frame

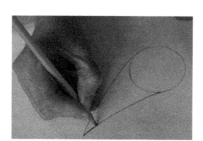

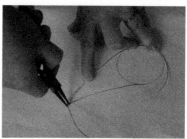

1. Using 1.0mm wire, follow the line of the pattern to make the teardrop shape.
   (**Tip:** Try to join the wire on a straight section rather than a curve or point as this will enable you to manipulate the shape and hide the join.)

2. Cut the wire, allowing a 5cm overlap.
3. Thread a needle with no more than 30cm of 0.4mm wire, double it on the needle so you are working with a 15cm length and knot the end.
4. Hook on and bind the wires as explained in 'Making simple wire bases' in Chapter 3.

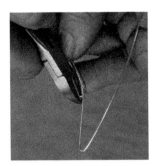

5. Cut the 0.4mm wire close to the frame with flat-back wire cutters. The closer you cut to the frame, the neater and safer your finished piece will be.

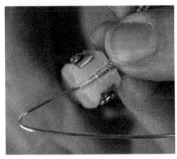

6. Smooth off the cut end with nylon jaw pliers.

Making the fabric for the frame

1. Unravel 0.2mm wire from the reel, gathering and loosely scrunching the wire as you go to create a random 'scribble' effect. (**Tip:** Try to keep the end visible or you may take some time trying to find it again at the end (as I did!))
2. Keep scrunching to create a dense area of wire that will cover the teardrop shape.
3. Unroll an extra 50cm of wire, then cut off the reel. Use this 50cm length of wire to stitch through the scrunched wire to help hold it together.

4. Take the cut end and, using a pair of round-nose pliers, roll the end to hide it in the scrunched wire and make it safe.

5. Thread a needle with a 60cm length of 0.2mm wire, double it on the needle so you are working with a 30cm length and knot the end. Begin overstitching to the frame, looping back through the knot to secure. Start at the join, tucking in any excess wire as you go round.

To decorate

1. Group a bunch of feathers and hold them together by wrapping them in 0.2mm wire at the base.

2. Wrap the feathers with wire and add feathers by layering them on top of each other, then stitch into each feather with wire.

3. Stitch to the top of the teardrop on the back of the frame, passing wire stitches between the feathers as well as around to weave them together.

4. I have also added a mixture of metal and coloured glass beads to the piece. Sew them on to the base randomly using 0.2mm wire.

To finish, line the piece as described in 'Kathleen' in Chapter 7 and attach a comb and grip wire as described in Chapter 3.

This is another variation on the scrunched shape, proving that any shape is possible using this method.

Working with Knitted Wire and Cup Chain

This Chapter focuses on my most exciting and interesting find.

When I was first introduced to pre-made knitted wire in 2009, I was fascinated (excuse the pun) by the fact I had never seen it before except in a larger version used as chain mail in the 1991 film *Robin Hood: Prince of Thieves*, which I worked on.

I can't tell you how much this fabric has revolutionised my tiara-making. It is so versatile and allows some of my more outlandish designs to come alive.

I started to use it to make flowers, then I began using it to extend combs, then included it in bases. Now it is part and parcel of many of my tiaras.

Enjoy the versatility of this fabric.

I wanted to make a statement piece for this Chapter. I have dedicated it to my mother, Kathleen; I wanted it to be special, as she was to me. This project is a good example of using ready-made pieces that can be collated and arranged to make a stunning wedding headdress.

Materials needed

1.0mm wire for base

85mm wide 0.1mm tight knit wire

85mm wide 0.2mm coarse knitted wire

0.4mm wire for binding

0.2mm wire for sewing

2 diamante flower strips – also known as cup chain (15cm x 65mm from BDi)

Marquise clasp fastener (I used JR05344 from Josy Rose)

Ready-set stones from EIMASS to fill in if needed

8cm comb

Tools needed

Acetate film	Double-sided sticky tape	Poly pocket plastic file
Photocopier/printer-scanner	Flat-back wire cutters	Craft scissors
Straw/milliners' needles, size 6	Long glass-headed pins	Round-nose pliers
Compressed foam mat		

Beginner/intermediate level   *Time taken: 2-3 hours depending on shape and frame*

This piece demonstrates a lovely way to incorporate jewellery pieces into your headdresses, perhaps a piece of old paste jewellery or, as in this example, a belt clip. Before you begin, bear in mind that the backs of some of your pieces may need some support to keep them stable when placing onto your frame for sewing.

Making the frame

1. Arrange the pieces of cup chain to form your design. Take time to work out ways they might fit with each other. Photocopy your work for reference as described in 'Creating a design guide', Chapter 3.
2. Use the photocopy to measure and shape the 1.0mm wire for the outline. Cut the wire, allowing a 5cm overlap, and join as described in 'Making simple wire bases' in Chapter 3.

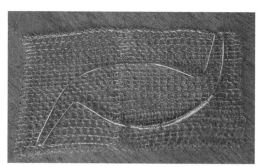

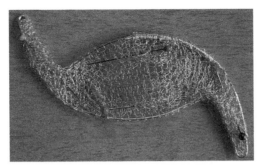

3. Cut a piece of 85mm wide 0.2mm coarse knitted wire slightly bigger than your frame. Stretch diagonally and slide the shape into the wire tube. Finish off by folding the raw edges into the tube.

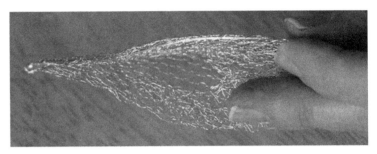

4. Tuck in the corners and shape to fit the frame. Overstitch to the frame using 0.2mm wire and a Straw/milliners' needle. Thread a size 6 Straw/milliners' needle with no more than 60cm of 0.2mm wire, double it on the needle so you are working with a 30cm length and knot the end.

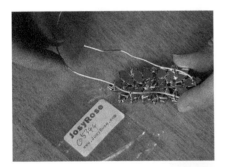
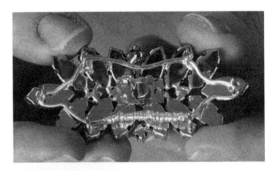

5. Next comes wiring the central piece of the design. Begin by checking your central piece to make sure all clamps are bent securely over each stone; use round-nose pliers to fix any loose stones. Because this is a belt clip (a hooked clip that comes in two parts, used as a feature on a slim belt for bridal and evening wear), the clasp must be pushed down to keep it closed. A supporting frame of 1.0mm wire is made by threading through the loops already on the back of this piece. Overlap and bind the wires in the same way as for the base.

6. Working on a soft surface such as a compressed foam mat, pin the cup chain pieces to the covered frame, reshaping the frame as you go. You will find the cup chain has a natural curve and will bend more one way than the other (see above picture). Follow the natural curve and match up the design at each end.

7. Thread a needle with no more than 60cm of 0.2mm wire, double it on the needle so you are working with a 30cm length and knot the end.
8. Working from one end, stitch into the frame, then bind between the stones in the cup chain. Squeeze the frame as you stitch to hide it behind the cup chain.
9. As you reach the end, line up the second piece of cup chain and bind over to hold in place.

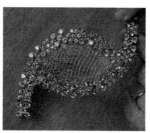

10. Begin attaching the second piece of cup chain, starting as shown in the photograph so the two pieces can be matched up at both ends.

11. Push the middle of the frame up to create room for the central piece.

12. Push the loops of the central piece through the knitted wire and sew from the reverse side, using both the loops and the frame you attached for support to secure the piece in place.

13. If you feel your piece has gaps, consider attaching individual stones.
    (**Tip:** Don't mix glass and acrylic as it makes the piece look poorly designed and of low quality).

Lining the frame

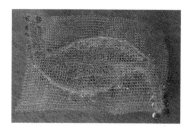 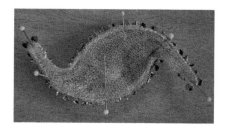

1. Take a piece of 85mm wide 0.1mm tight knit wire and cut a piece that is slightly bigger than the frame. Turn in all the cut ends and shape the knitted wire to the frame. You may need to stretch and pull this into shape.
2. Thread a needle with 60cm of 0.2mm wire, double it on the needle so you are working with a 30cm length and knot the end. Sew the backing to the frame with either an overstitch or a slip stitch. Either stitch is good for this.
3. Attach the comb as shown in Chapter 3.

Siobhan wants to make tiaras for a living in the future. She has attended various courses including my tiara-making, birdcage veil and flower-making courses.

Siobhan said:

I feel more confident tackling unusual shapes now. The instructions and photos were really clear for a beginner. Making the wire frame was the most difficult part; I made mine a little too wide. How do I adjust this?

Denise said:

You can overcome problems with the frame by squeezing it gently and using individual stones to fill the gaps.

This is a fantastic example of a diadem piece. A diadem is an upright post of diamante with additional diamante on either side. This style originated in the medieval era. The central post is always higher than any decoration on either side of the tiara. This style of tiara or crown was also worn by medieval men.

Materials needed

1.0mm wire for frame   0.4mm wire for binding

0.2mm wire for sewing

2m of 15mm wide 0.1mm tight knit wire

0.5m of 4mm silver cup chain   All-purpose adhesive

Ready-set stones (I used 8mm, 7mm and 6.5mm from EIMASS)

2 x 1.25mm jump rings (silver-plated copper)

1m of 0.5cm wide satin cream or hair-coloured ribbon

Small comb, five-pronged

Tools needed

Flat-back wire cutters   Craft scissors   Nylon jaw pliers

Long glass-headed pins   Straw/milliners' needle, size 6   Compressed foam

Intermediate/advanced   Time taken: 3–5 hours depending on decoration

The picture shows two types of chain: one backed in cotton and one backed in metal. These are attached to a frame by sewing with 0.2mm wire. The cotton-backed chain can be stitched through the cotton webbing, whereas the metal-backed chain needs overstitching twice because the 0.2mm wire can break easily when sewing over it.

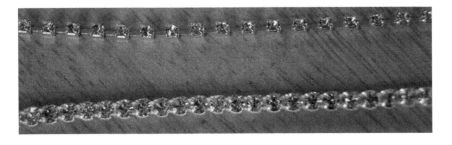

Making the frame

1. Design your shape as described in 'Creating a design guide' in Chapter 3.
   (**Tip:** Make sure that the highest point is central in your design and not too tall.)
2. Use your design to measure and shape the 1.0mm wire for the outline. Allow a 15cm overlap and join by wrapping with 0.4mm wire as shown in 'Making a simple wire base' in Chapter 3.

Covering the frame

1. Cut three 10cm lengths of 15mm wide 0.1mm ultra-fine knitted wire tube.
2. Thread two of the 10cm lengths over the arms of the frame (one length over each arm) until they meet in the middle.
3. Thread the final 10cm length over the diadem (central post).

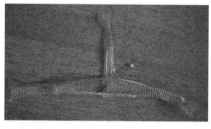

4. Pin all three lengths of the knitted wire tube so that they meet in the centre and the knitted wire covers the whole frame.

5. Stretch each length of the knitted wire tube to make it taut over the frame.

6. At the end of each arm, twist the knitted wire tube fabric to hold the knitted wire in place. Measure 2.5cm of the knitted wire tube beyond the end of the frame, which you will need to make a seam. Trim off the excess.

7. At the top of the diadem, twist the knitted wire tube. (**Tip**: As the diadem is the main focus of this tiara it is worth lining it with knitted wire.)
8. Measure the height of the diadem. Double this measurement and add 1cm to the total, then trim off the excess knitted wire tube.
9. Thread a size 6 Straw/milliners' needle with no more than 60cm of 0.2mm wire, double it on the needle so you are working with a 30cm length and knot the end.
10. Sew around the frame. To begin, knot the end and cast on the underside, tucking any cut ends back in on the same side to neaten. Continue to overstitch around the frame, taking care to stitch through all the layers of knitted wire at the centre. Remember to leave additional knitted wire at the end of the diadem to use as a lining.

11. Smooth over all the edges with the handles of a pair of scissors to make sure there are no sharp ends sticking out.

Trimming the frame

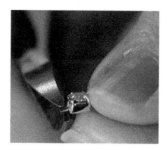

Tip: The ends of the cup chain have a metal bar that joins each stone and clamp together. The excess part of the metal bar will need to be trimmed off.

1. Use long pins to pin between the cup chain bars. Finish the decoration with a stone on the edge for a professional finish.

2. Sew the stones to the frame using 60cm of 0.2mm wire wire, doubled on the needle so you are working with a 30cm length with a knot on the end.

3. Cast on at one end with 0.2mm wire. Stitch on the edge of the frame, passing through the frame and between each stone, keeping the first row of stones on the edge of the frame. Use one or two stitches between each stone, depending on how far apart the stones on your chain are.

4. Keep adding rows of the cup chain until you have covered the two arms – but not the diadem. Use your choice of small ready-set stones to fill in any spaces that you may have.

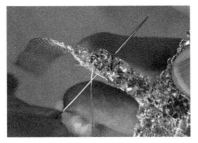

5. Fill in the diadem with single ready-set stones. Make sure you start from the top of the diadem with the smallest stones and work down to the bottom of the diadem where you will need to place the largest stones.

6. Fasten the two end stones to the frame with a dab of clear adhesive glue.

Lining and making the extension of the frame

1. Take a 25cm piece of 15mm knitted wire and fold in half lengthways. Unfold and line up the centre of the knitted wire (the fold) with the centre of the diadem.

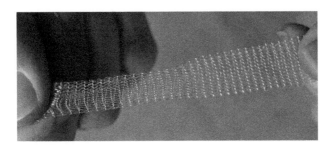

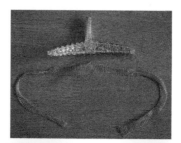

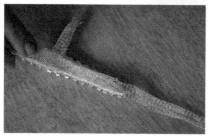

2. Fold the diadem lining down and tuck behind the 25cm length of 15mm knitted wire.

3. Pin the knitted wire and the lining to the frame. Depending on the size of your frame, this will leave approximately 5cm of knitted wire beyond the end of each arm of the frame.

4. Cast on a 60cm length of 0.2mm wire folded in half so you are working with a 30cm length and overstitch the lining to the underside of your frame.

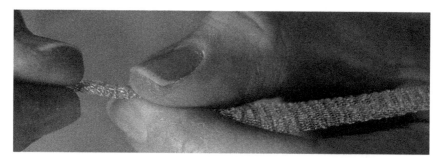

5. Roll the knitted wire at the end of each arm between your fingers to create a chain. Make sure that these lengths are equal.

6. Sew approximately 5cm of cup chain to cover the knitted wire chain.

7. Thread one 1.25mm copper jump ring onto each end of the knitted wire. Fold and stitch into your knitted wire using 0.2mm wire.

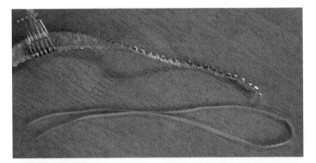

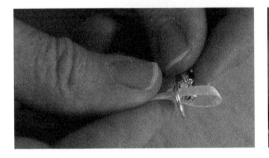
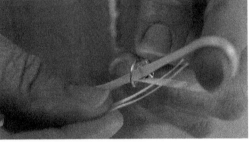

8. Take a 50cm length of 5mm ribbon. Cut the ends to form points. Fold in half lengthways and thread through the loop as described under 'Ribbon loops' in Chapter 3.

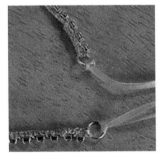

Chapter 8

Broken Jewellery, Brooches and Buttons

Many brides have asked me to incorporate something into the tiara or headdress because it was Granny's and they wanted her to be represented at the wedding. I have managed to incorporate buttons, brooches and belt hooks into headdress designs. Even a freshwater pearl that 'Grandpa found on the beach' has been added on request.

The 'less is more' mantra really applies to this Chapter. Avoid cheap and nasty plastic and foil pieces (unless they have huge sentimental value); they may be cheap but they look it! As my mum used to say, 'You can't make a silk purse out of a pig's ear.'

As well as family heirloom pieces that I've been asked to incorporate, I have also added pieces from antique fairs, car boot sales and flea markets. These, on occasion, can turn out to be the star of your collection.

Helen (small hair combs)

This style is ideal for brides who want very little decoration in their hair. It is made by using two very cheap brooch pieces that can be found in a bargain store.

Materials needed

  30cm of 15mm wide 0.1mm tight knit wire
  2 six-prong combs
  0.2mm wire for sewing
  2 brooches (I used a squared-off small brooch,
    £1.99, 4cm x 3cm)

Tools needed

Craft scissors   Straw/milliners' needles, size 6   Flat-back wire cutters

Beginner level   Time taken: less than 1½ hour

1. Cover the top bar of a small six-prong comb with 10cm of the tight knit wire. Wrap around the comb widthways, covering the front and back, and turning in all excess and ends.

2. Unpin the brooch and pin onto the knitted wire, positioning the brooch so the pin is level with the top of the comb (where the knitted wire is sewn).

3. Loop a stitch and sew one stitch to anchor the wire at the bottom of the comb where the brooch lies.

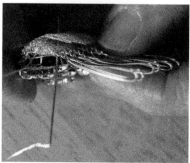

4. Cut 5cm of the tight knit wire and turn in the raw edges. Using 0.2mm wire (and the size 6 Straw/milliners' needle), attach the knitted wire to the back of the brooch to cover the pin and stitching.

Combs are notoriously hard to keep in your hair. Using this simple tip you can keep a headdress in the finest of hair with a comb.

1. Take a piece of the bride's hair from the point where you are placing the headdress. Split the strands of hair, taking a piece of the top layer, and set it aside.
2. Cross pin over the hair on the head, even curl loops of hair and cross clip that hair.
3. Lay the set-aside hair over the top of the cross pins to disguise what you have done.
4. Now push the comb behind the cross pins; the headdress will grip the pins and stay safely in the hair.

At some point all milliners will need to make a decorated hair pin. As this is currently very popular, it is a good skill to have. These are quick and easy and allow you to extend the pins so you can add more decoration to your designs.

Materials needed

4 looped hair pins (to make a set of two pins)   15mm wide 0.1mm tight knit wire

0.2mm wire for sewing   0.4mm wire for wrapping

2 brooches (approximately 4cm x 2cm)

Tools needed

Tape measure/ruler   Craft scissors   Long glass-headed pins
Straw/milliners' needle, size 6   Flat-back wire cutters

Beginner/intermediate level   *Time taken: under 1½ hours*

1. Cut a 12cm length of 0.4mm wire. Match together the end loops of two of the hair pins and slide the wire through the two overlapping loops. Wrap to fix them together. Be careful not to catch your wire on any of the other hair pin loops or it will affect the alignment. Twist the two ends of the wire together and cut off any excess; bend the cut ends to the inside to make safe.

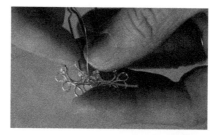

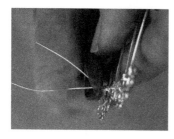

2. Using a 10cm length of the knitted wire, wrap around the top of the hair pins widthways, covering the front and back, and turning in all excess and ends. Pin in place.

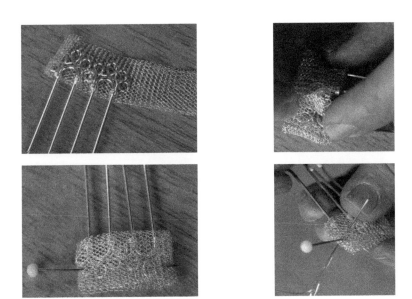

3. Cut a 60cm length of the 0.2mm wire. Thread onto a size 6 Straw/milliners' needle, double the wire over and tie a knot in the end (so you have a 30cm length of double wire). Hide the knotted end inside the knitted wire. Fold in any sharp corners as you overstitch around the edge of the knitted wire. Finish with several stab stitches through the middle, passing through the loops on the pins. This will provide you with a base to stitch into and should feel quite solid at this point.

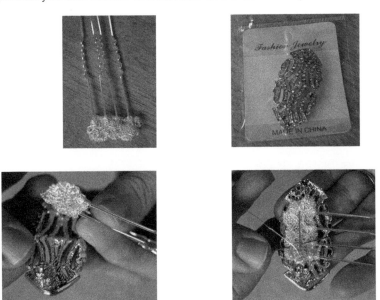

4. Open the brooch and use the pin to attach to the knitted-wire-covered hair pins. Close the fastener and centralise the brooch.

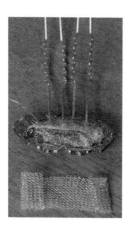 

5. Take another length of knitted wire to cover over the back. Neaten the ends and stitch in place with 0.2mm wire.

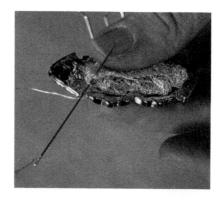

Helen, a working mum, loves crafts, especially knitting and crochet. Knowing her attention to detail, which has been a huge help when proofreading this book, I was relieved to find she found the instructions nice and clear and the pictures helpful.

Helen said:

I loved doing these pieces. I was a bit hesitant about sewing with wire, but honestly if you can sew a button on a shirt then you can do this! I can't believe I've gone from never having done anything like this before to making a lovely hair piece in about an hour and a half.

Another way of using this method was devised by someone else who has not been on any of our courses. Julie Moth is a working mum and crafter, and loves crochet.

Julie used the same method as Helen to make her hair pieces but has adapted it to use with combs.:

Julie said:

I found it easy to follow the methods and was confident to change the hair attachment. One thing I found was that using Denise's tips helped me to understand how I could adapt to using a comb.

Chapter 9
Hair Vines

This is a tricky subject and is limited in the effect it can achieve; however, after a ten-year gap in tiara-making it's one of the first methods I tried and, as far as I am concerned, if it is done correctly, it can look divine on a head. The hair vine has made a recent comeback, with designers piling on more trimmings than ever, so a lot of skills are needed to design a perfect vine.

A hair vine is a collection of wires or ribbons that are either twisted or fixed together with intermittent decoration that can be shown in the hair. Flowers and loose wires with beads are traditional, but now makers are using metal plate and large stones.

This headdress was first seen in Ancient Greek times, known as 'fillet' of ribbon, and was encrusted with jewels and metal plate. Now seen on ITV's *Victoria*, it is a fashion statement that is set to get popular.

In this Chapter you will learn to make a proper hair vine and a twist on the hair vine, a forehead-headband, as worn by some of the actresses in *Downton Abbey*.

Polly (flower hair vine)

The advent of 'festival life' in the summer gives us a new wave of hippy chic, country-looking wedding headdresses. I have chosen to include one in this headdress book because of its rising popularity. The method I have chosen is quick and easy and the result looks very professional. Say 'goodbye' to the long lengths of multiple wires that make a vine; say 'hello' to the marvellous use of perl, an old, traditional embroiderer's couching made from tubular coiled wire.

Materials needed for the vine

Perl or bullion size 1.9

0.4mm or 0.6mm wire (depending on which size will go through your perl or bullion)

0.2mm wire for binding and sewing

1.60mm jump ring

Materials needed to decorate

Paper roses, 3 large, 6 small

6 silk gypsophila flowers

0.2mm wire for binding and sewing

15mm wide 0.1mm tight knit wire

Tools needed

Tape measure	Craft scissors
Flat-back wire cutters	Pencil or piece of 5mm dowel
Straw/milliners' needles, size 6	Nylon jaw pliers
Round-nose pliers	Long glass-headed pins

Intermediate/advanced level   *Time taken: 2–3 hours depending on decoration*

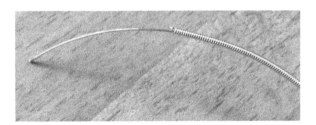

1. Take a 33cm length of perl wire and a 35cm length of 0.6mm wire (or 0.4mm wire; see the vine materials list). Be careful not to stretch the perl when measuring as this is easy to do!

2. Thread the 0.6mm wire through the perl wire until the ends pop out; you should have 1cm of wire bare at each end.

Making the end loops

These loops allow the vine to grip the wearer's hair and are a very handy addition to the vine.

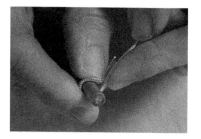
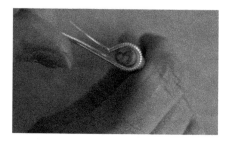

1. Bend the end of the wire over a thin pencil or piece of dowel (5mm) until it looks like a crook; make sure that your loop includes the perl wire too.

2. Push a glass-headed pin (longer and thicker than a standard pin) inside the perl and open the coil wide enough to push the end of the hooked wire in. This creates the loop at the end of your vine.

3. Thread a needle with no more than 60cm of 0.2mm wire, double it on the needle so you are working with a 30cm length and knot the end. Hook it onto a perl groove. Wrap the perl and the wires together, tightening as you go. Repeat on the other end.

 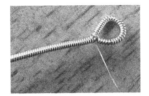 

Decorating the vines

As you start adding the flowers to the vine, checking their position on a head mannequin is advisable. Some customers will have a strong preference for where the decoration sits, so measurements taken at the beginning of your fitting can be crucial to the final look of the hair vine.

1. Cut each of the flowers, layering the length of the flower stems. For example, the first flower stem length is cut to 2cm, the second 4cm and the third 6cm.
2. Starting with the shortest flower, attach each flower separately by binding it to the vine with 0.2mm wire; I have used a 60cm length folded in half to make 30cm. Smooth and cut ends with nylon jaw pliers before lining. I have layered the stems one on top of the other. Anything else added to the vine must be graduated in this way to avoid bulk and weight.

Tip: Never twist the flower stem wires directly onto the vine or two things will happen:

a. Any twisting of flower stems will weaken the wire and the flower will probably fall apart; the head will detach from the stem. The wire from ready-made flowers is usually a soft wire and it easily breaks.
b. Twisting the stem wire onto the perl vine will add too much bulk and create uneven lumps on the vine.

To line the hair vine (perl wire)

1. Take an 8cm piece of 15mm wide 0.1mm tight knit wire; fold in 0.5cm each end.
2. Using the glass-headed pins, wrap the knitted wire over the cut ends of flower wire which are on your perl hair vine, pinning as you go, making sure to cover over any untidy wires.

3. Thread a size 6 Straw/milliners' needle with 60cm of 0.2mm wire, double it on the needle so you are working with a 30cm length and knot the end.
4. Sew the knitted wire to the vine, making sure that you cover all the wrapping and wires.

5. Repeat this over any parts of the hair vine you have bound and sewn to.

6. Add a jump ring to the back of the central flower (on the vine) to create an extra gripping point for pinning into the hair.

Lucy Bowler, one of my regular students, has taken the British School of Millinery's Beginner's, Intermediate and Advanced courses, which take a year to complete in total, and graduated from us in summer 2016. She has also taken Tiara 1 & 2, so she has a basic knowledge of making wired headdresses.

Lucy's Vine on her daughter Annie

Lucy is pictured here with a Giffords Circus performer wearing one of Lucy's hats, which she made on one of our courses.

Lucy said:

I really enjoyed making the hair vine and think it's an adaptable piece. I am looking forward to coming up with my own designs.

Lucy asked:

I loved decorating this vine with the flowers; is it possible to decorate the vine with other bridal fabrics?

Denise's answer:

Of course! I have made vines with metal pieces, lace and even waxed flowers. This process lends itself to all types of trimmings. Just see the pictures of other vines I have made; here they are . . .

1920s headbands have been the fashion for years, and more recently the TV show *Downton Abbey* has spurred a new craze in this type of headband.

This was one of the first headdresses I made with the knitted wire. I was amazed by how quick it was to make and how easy it was to produce and decorate this headband.

Materials for the main band

15mm wide 0.1mm tight knit wire

0.2mm wire to sew with, same colour as knitted wire

Sew-on backed Swarovski stones or sew-on crystals (obtained from EIMASS):

13 x 8mm backed stones	2 x 5mm backed stones
2 x 2mm silver beads	4mm crystal droplet roundel

Materials for the finished ends

2 metal beads, 9mm, large bore (i.e. with a big hole) and complementing the look of the knitted wire

2 bicorn crystals, 4mm	2 metal beads, 2mm

Tools needed

Tape measure/ruler	Craft scissors
Long glass-headed pins	Straw/milliners' needles, size 6
Flat-back wire cutters Nylon jaw pliers	

Intermediate level   Time taken: 2–3 hours

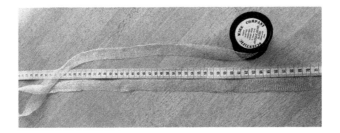

1. Measure out 70cm of the knitted wire and cut with the craft scissors.

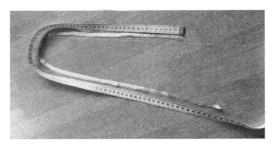

2. Gently stretch the knitted wire lengthwise until it is 1cm wide.

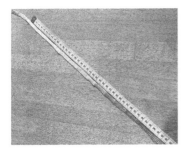

3. Using 0.2mm wire, mark the centre of the knitted wire with a tacking marker. This is a piece of wire sewn into the knitted wire to indicate where the stones will be sewn. (**Tip:** Pins will fall out of knitted wire, so it is easier to use a piece of wire as a tacking marker.)

4. Working out from the centre, place a tacking marker every 3cm until you have six each side, making thirteen markers in total.

5. Working from the centre, start to sew the ready-backed stones or crystals onto the band again using a 0.2mm wire. If you are not using ready-backed stones, please see 'Setting stones' in Chapter 3 for how to set stones into the sew-on backs.

6. To add the droplet below the centre stone, thread a needle with no more than 40cm of 0.2mm wire, double it on the needle so you are working with a 20 cm length and knot the end. Thread on the two 2mm silver beads, then thread on the crystal droplet roundel. Take the thread back up through the silver beads and back into the knitted wire, pull tight and secure with a few more stitches. Sew the smaller stones either side of the centre stone.

7. Because this bandeau is worn close to the forehead it is to the wearer's benefit to line this piece. Take a piece of 15mm wide 0.1mm tight knit wire; I used a size that fits the sewing done on the band. Stretch a piece to 41cm. Turn in 1cm each end to make the lining tidy.

8. Thread a size 6 Straw/milliners' needle with no more than 60cm of 0.2mm wire, double it on the needle so you are working with a 30cm length and knot the end.

9. Cast on and overstitch the outside edge, catching the lining and the front of the bandeau together.

10. Roll the ends of the knitted wire so it tapers into a cord. Fold each end over by 0.5cm to hem each end separately and sew each hem down with 0.2mm wire. Thread through a large bore bead that complements the end of the knitted wire.

11. Thread a needle with no more than 30cm of 0.2mm wire, double it on the needle so you are working with a 15cm length and knot the end.

12. Cast on to the end of the knitted wire and thread through a bicorn crystal and a 2mm metal bead, then take the thread back through the bicorn and secure onto the knitted wire, pulling tight and securing with a few more stitches. Use the excess wire to bind the ends. Cover these stitches by sliding the large bead back over

Here are some alternative styles for finishing the ends of the rolled wire.

Here I show using a diamante button with a shank and mini sew-on crystals (obtained from ElMASS).

Example of a small diamante stone sewn on the ends

Two examples of using diamante buttons to finish the ends

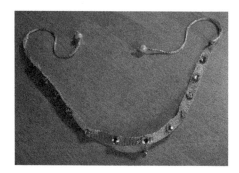

Sophia Spicer ('Beetle' to her friends) has been a student on the British School of Millinery's Beginner's, Intermediate and Advanced courses, graduating from us in summer 2016. She has also taken Tiara 1 class with me and had a basic knowledge of making wired headdresses before attempting this project, but she was not used to using knitted wire.

Beetle said:

I took a while to get used to using the knitted wire. I found the wire kinked whilst sewing and using the knitted wire takes getting used to.

Beetle asked:

I did not make the ties on the end of the band long enough. Is there a way you can rectify this mistake?

Denise's answer:

Yes. Cut off the ends of the knitted wire, after the last stones; leave enough to turn the knitted wire under and finish neatly. When you add lining, add the length of two ties extra to the lining. Finish the headband as per the instructions.

Brands

A heartfelt thank-you goes to the following brands, which had faith that I would do their goods justice. Thank you!

Bodega: http://www.bodegawomenswear.com/

Cocoa Couture: http://www.cocoacouture.co.uk/

Cowley Manor Hotel: http://www.cowleymanor.com/

Frilly Chantilly: http://www.frillychantilly.co.uk/

Outsider: http://www.outsiderfashion.com/

Russell & Bromley: http://www.russellandbromley.co.uk/

Flowers: Kopend Creations: http://www.kopendcreations.co.uk/

Children's dresses made by Denise Innes-Spencer for her own bridesmaids at her wedding.

Suppliers List

Item	Supplier
All-purpose glue	Hobbycraft
Bicorn iridescent (AB) crystals/tools	Creative Beadcraft
Feathers Combs Metal Headbands	The Trimmings Company
Diamante metal pieces	Imagine DIY
Flat-back wire cutters	Hobbycraft
Straw/milliners' needles	Hobbycraft
Knitted wire	The Scientific Wire Company
Nylon jaw pliers	Creative Beadcraft/EIMASS
Ready-made headband	Parkin Fabrics
Round-nose pliers	Hobbycraft
Scissors	Hobbycraft
Silver bullion/tools	The Scientific Wire Company
Wire (all gauges)	Creative Beadcraft/The Scientific Wire Company
Beaded diamante pieces	Barnet Lawson Trimmings

Supplier details

Ellie Rose Flowers: https://www.ellierose

Creative Beadcraft: https://www.creativebeadcraft.co.uk/

EIMASS: http://www.eimass.co.uk/

The Scientific Wire Company: https://www.scientificwire.com/

Imagine DIY: http://www.imaginediy.co.uk/

The Trimmings Company: https://www.thetrimmingscompany.co.uk

Hobbycraft: http://www.hobbycraft.co.uk/

Josie Rose www.josierose.com

Barnet Lawson Trimmings: www.bltrimmings.com

Handcrafted Card Company: www.thehandcraftedcardcompany.co.uk

Bibliography

de Courtais, Georgine. *Women's Hats, Headdresses and Hairstyles.* Dover Publications, 2006

Munn, Geoffrey. *Tiaras Past and Present.* V&A, 2002

Smith, Rodney, and Leslie Smolan. *The Hat Book.* Doubleday, 1993

Tortora, Phyllis G, and Robert S Merkel. *Fairchild's Dictionary of Textiles.* 7th edition. Fairchild, 2009

Turner Wilcox, R. *The Mode in Hats and Headdress: A Historical Survey with 190 Plates.* Dover Publications, 2008

Books

Oxford Dictionary

Acknowledgements

We worked on this book.

Models

Fiona Campbell   Amelia Black   Lisa Moulder-Jenkins   Rhiannon Parker

Child models

Louise Fisher   Rachel Fisher   Cerys Wright

Hair

Nykita Jowsey with permission of Laura Leigh Hairdressing, Cheltenham

Trudi Seddon with permission of Me Hair Beauty & Barbers, Cheltenham

Make-up

Sophie Everett

Photography

Emily McMahon, Frozen Visions

Fashion stylist and PR

Heidi Sweeting

Assistants to Heidi Sweeting

Eliza Abel-Smith   Natasha Scahill

Assistant to Denise and curriculum advisor

Sue Fisher

Sample tester and making assistant

Gemma Sangwine

Assistant

Helen Bond

Fetching and carrying

Richard Spencer

Illustrations in the book

Susie Pitcher   Angela Torr   Denise Innes-Spencer

Editors

Gillian Haslam   Richard Spencer   Harriet Evans

I have used other pictures from previous publications; here are the credits for those.

Additional photographs

Cotswold Style and Paul Bates

Spencer McPherson of Still Moving Media

Annie Johnston   Helen Lee

Hand Shots photography

Gemma Sangwine, Denise Innes Spencer and Richard Spencer

Make-up artist and hair

Denise Lowe

Gowns

Jayne Bolton   Suzanne Neville

Students

In order to write a book that students would want to use, I think it's good to hear what other students' experiences were.

When people ring me up to find out about our courses I always refer them to other students who have taken the courses. They will tell you if they have not liked it. Luckily for me, they always tell the truth. Which is why I felt that the students would be the best advocate for the projects in this book.

The following students helped by sampling the projects before the book went to print.

Becky Jeal, Tewkesbury   Siobhan Goodman, Berkshire

Nicky Reading, Cheltenham   Helen Bond, Cheltenham

Julie Moth, Bishops Cleeve   Gemma Sangwine, Stroud

Sophia 'Beetle' Spicer, Marlborough   Lucy Bowler, Oxford

Irene Spencer, Bolton

If I have missed anyone from this book, I can put it right; please get in touch with me and I will include you in the text on the next reprint.

I welcome your feedback on this, my first book.

Please contact me at:

info@thebritishschoolofmillinery.com

Further Thanks

My thanks go to Richard, Faith, Isobel and Megan, my sister Pauline and all the extended family who have put up with me the past few months (and years), whilst I was writing this book.

Thanks to my dedicated friends Sue and Helen, who pick me up whenever I see them.

Big thank you to Tracy Connop and Bridget Bailey, who kindly wrote such wonderful forewords.

To all the dedicated students who keep coming back to try out new courses and those who took time to test some of the projects for the book, thank you!

To all the people who worked on this book, especially Becky from *HATalk* and Miles and his team at the Choir Press, thank you!

Also the army of friends that are fondly known as the 'Hatherley Ladies'. I know their prayers were with me because here is the book! Thank you!

I could not have done this without any of you!

Final words are in memory of my mother Kathleen Gabrielle Constable, a beautiful Irish angel, who by God's grace is up in heaven at His side. Her favourite toast, right back at you, Mum:

May the road rise to meet you,

May the wind be always on your back,

May the sun shine warm upon your face,

And rains fall soft upon your fields,

And until we meet again,

May God hold you in the hollow of his hand.

Slainte! ('Cheers' in Gaelic.)

Denise Innes-Spencer has been a traditional milliner for twenty-four years. She gained a BA with Honours from Middlesex University, is a qualified teacher of millinery and fashion and has taught at universities all over the world.

She started her creative career as the head of ladies' hats at Bermans and Nathans, the world-renowned costumiers. After a long career in television, film and theatre she was snapped up by the bridal wear designer Suzanne Neville. Their partnership lasted ten years.

After a brief spell teaching at various universities and colleges she founded the British School of Millinery, which she still runs today. She has supported Professor Roger Kneebone of Imperial College London's research into dexterity skills.

Denise still makes headwear for brides and their wedding parties, and has been featured in many bridal and fashion magazines.

She lives in the Cotswolds with her husband Richard and their children Faith, Isobel and Megan.